SPIRITS

OF THE

TAROT

From The Cups' Abundance to The Magician's Creation,
78 COCKTAIL RECIPES INSPIRED BY THE TAROT

THEA ENGST

ADAMS MEDIA

NEW YORK   LONDON   TORONTO   SYDNEY   NEW DELHI

Adams Media
An Imprint of Simon & Schuster, Inc.
100 Technology Center Drive
Stoughton, Massachusetts 02072

First Adams Media hardcover edition February 2023

ADAMS MEDIA and colophon are trademarks of Simon & Schuster.

For information about special discounts for bulk purchases, please contact Simon & Schuster Special Sales at 1-866-506-1949 or business@simonandschuster.com.

The Simon & Schuster Speakers Bureau can bring authors to your live event. For more information or to book an event contact the Simon & Schuster Speakers Bureau at 1-866-248-3049 or visit our website at www.simonspeakers.com.

Interior design by Sylvia McArdle
Illustrations by Emma Taylor
Photographs by Harper Point Photography
Tarot card illustrations from the Rider–Waite Tarot Deck by A.E. Waite, illustrated by Pamela Colman Smith, first published in 1909 by The Rider Company Ltd.

Manufactured in China

10 9 8 7 6 5 4 3 2 1

Library of Congress Cataloging-in-Publication Data
Names: Engst, Thea, author.
Title: Spirits of the tarot / Thea Engst.
Description: First Adams Media hardcover edition. | Stoughton, Massachusetts: Adams Media, 2023 | Includes index.
Identifiers: LCCN 2022035042 | ISBN 9781507219850 (hc) | ISBN 9781507219867 (ebook)
Subjects: LCSH: Cocktails. | Tarot. | LCGFT: Cookbooks.
Classification: LCC TX951 .E5825 2023 | DDC 641.87/4--dc23/eng/20220806
LC record available at https://lccn.loc.gov/2022035042

ISBN 978-1-5072-1985-0
ISBN 978-1-5072-1986-7 (ebook)

DEDICATION

For Nana, my first bar guest.

CONTENTS

Introduction . . . 11

CHAPTER 5
MINOR ARCANA: SUIT OF CUPS ... 93

CHAPTER 6
MINOR ARCANA: SUIT OF PENTACLES ... 115

CHAPTER 7
MINOR ARCANA: SUIT OF SWORDS ... 139

CHAPTER 8

THE MAJOR ARCANA RECIPES... 163

ACKNOWLEDGMENTS

---◆---

This book would not be possible without the support of my soul sister, Eileen Mullan, whose belief in my abilities knows no bounds. Eileen: The feeling is mutual; thank you.

I'd also like to thank my relentlessly supportive siblings: Lea, Lisbeth, Lauren, and Stefan. I don't know where I'd be without your love and laughter.

And to my nieces, my little witches: Jade and Ava, thank you for inspiring me to continue to create potions. Aunt Hippie Witch can't wait to see what you grow into.

Finally, to my parents, who raised me to love and trust nature: Thank you.

INTRODUCTION

A powerful mode of divination magic, tarot can open communication between you and your spirit guides, illuminating intuitive knowledge within. And now you can connect with your guides and celebrate their insights in a luscious new way! *Spirits of the Tarot* combines the mysticism of tarot with the delicious world of cocktails to help you embrace the wisdom of the cards with seventy-eight libations crafted in their image.

In Part 1, you'll delve deeper into the arts of tarot and bartending, from how to shuffle and draw cards to the bewitching flavors and intentional ingredients that bring magic to an ordinary mixed drink. And in Part 2, it's time to toast to a divinely inspired cocktail. Flip to the corresponding recipe for a drawn card, or whatever card calls to you, for a description and key themes of that card, along with simple steps for creating its potable embodiment. You can also choose from several recipes by pulling multiple cards. Organized in the Minor Arcana suits and Major Arcana cards, there are enticing potions for every palate.

Begin the journey signified by The Fool with a tasty Fool's Errand. Sip the bold flavors of The Warrior's Manhattan as you reflect on the self-empowering message of the Strength card. Share the romantic vibes of Aphrodite's Blessings with the one you love. And more.

And if you're feeling emboldened to stir up your own interpretations, flip to the end of the book to find an appendix of each tarot card and its meanings to guide your adventures.

Whether you are celebrating the abundance reflected in the Ace of Pentacles, setting an intention to embrace change with the Page of Wands, or simply looking for a special twist on your favorite martini, there is a corresponding cocktail to bring a little liquid magic to your experiences.

PART 1

THE WORLDS OF TAROT AND BARTENDING

The first step of blending the occult with mixed drinks is understanding a little bit more of the tarot. With tarot reading comes power, susceptibility, and strength, and you must prepare yourself adequately to perform thorough readings, while protecting yourself from being energetically drained. The first chapter in this part guides you through everything you need to know about tarot before doing a reading or crafting one of the drinks in Part 2. It features several spreads to learn how to read cards when reversed, how to trust yourself, and how to invite your guides in for help. You will also learn how to protect your energy, how to cleanse your space, and when to take a break, among other things.

The second step in your journey through divine cocktail mixing is understanding the basics of bartending. There are terms and techniques that come up often when making cocktails, as well as tools every bartender should have. In Chapter 2, you will find information about the equipment, glassware, and bartending techniques used in the recipes in Part 2, as well as an introduction to some integral spirits for crafting cocktails. And in Chapter 3, you'll explore how syrups and other special additions can elevate a cocktail and infuse it with ancient magic. This chapter includes easy recipes for the syrups, salts, sugars, and more that are used in Part 2.

CHAPTER 1

TAROT BASICS

Tarot reading has been featured in mainstream media in recent years, but it is far from a new practice. In fact, it has been around since the 1430s, and because of its span over time, cultures, traditions, and languages, the art of tarot reading has a huge breadth of techniques and interpretations. The most important thing to remember when practicing tarot is to trust yourself and your guides.

This chapter is an exercise in learning the cards and accepting the messages your guides and your intuition send you via the card you pull. Here, you will explore the Minor and Major Arcanas, understand how astrology connects to tarot, and learn the steps for doing a card reading. You will also take a closer look at the differences between suits, card numbers, and court cards in the Minor Arcana, as well as the journey that unfolds in the Major Arcana. While the drinks in the book were designed to be paired with a one-card spread, you will also find information about other popular tarot spreads that you may try beyond this book. Your journey into the divine world of tarot begins now.

THE ARCANAS

The most significant division in the tarot deck is between the Minor Arcana and the Major Arcana. There are fifty-six Minor Arcana cards, making up the bulk of the deck. The Minor Arcana represent smaller events and opportunities for growth in more specific ways than the Major Arcana cards. These specifics are determined both by your question and the suit of the card you pull. There are twenty-two Major Arcana cards to complete the deck. They represent the significant changes and life events that come your way.

The Minor Arcana

There are more Minor Arcana cards than Major Arcana because humans tend to have more bandwidth for smaller bursts of growth than larger growth. The Minor Arcana are building blocks or steps toward the Major Arcana. Each Queen of the Minor Arcana, for example, is a piece of what eventually becomes The Empress of the Major Arcana. The Queen of Cups is about intuition and emotions, the Queen of Pentacles is about financial stability, the Queen of Swords is about communication and perception, and the Queen of Wands is about strength and stability. While each of these is a desirable harmony to achieve, you must have all of them to experience true balance and happiness. Therefore, as you grow to become a Queen of each suit, you eventually combine and surpass them all to become The Empress. In that sense, you can see a true pattern of a call to grow as you study the tarot.

The Suits

The other division in the tarot deck is the suit categories, which make up the Minor Arcana. The four suits are Cups, Wands, Swords, and Pentacles. Each suit is numbered Ace through Ten and has four face cards: Pages, Knights, Queens, and Kings. While suits are featured in some of the Major Arcana, they are the focus of the Minor Arcana. Each suit is connected to a different element—water, fire, earth, or air—and therefore also to certain zodiac signs (more on the zodiac signs later in this chapter). Because of this, they each concern unique areas of your life.

- **The suit of Cups (water):** Cups concern human relationships and love, though they are not strictly romance cards. Depending on your question and the surrounding cards in your spread, this could be a romance, friendship, professional relationship, or familial relationship.
- **The suit of Wands (fire):** The Wands are a suit of ambition, movement, growth, and sexuality. Because they are ambitious cards, they are often career-related, but Wands can also be about personal growth and entering a new stage of your life, whether it's personal or professional. It all depends on where the card falls in your spread, what your question is, and the cards surrounding it.
- **The suit of Swords (air):** Overall, the Swords tend to be the most negative of the Minor Arcana suits. These cards relate to your consciousness, often pointing out mindsets that need to be changed. Pulling a Sword isn't necessarily a bad thing, depending on where it falls in the card spread and what surrounds it, but these cards tend to involve challenges.
- **The suit of Pentacles (earth):** Pentacles concern material things, money, and earthly rewards or losses. The higher the numbers of this suit, the more wealth and financial stability they represent. Of course, there are struggles and challenges in this suit as well: Nothing comes for free or easily.

The Number Cards

The Minor Arcana suits each start with an Ace card rather than a One. The Ace is followed by Two and progresses to Ten before transitioning to the face cards. Aces represent new beginnings and gifts, Twos are all about some kind of a life balance, and Threes are group focused and often relate to a team project. Like the four walls of a home, Fours are all about stability, whether it's the financial stability of the Pentacles or the emotional stability of the Cups. Fives follow that stability with an indication of struggle and conflict. Pulling a Five signifies an argument, a confrontation, or a disconnect that comes from being unable to find a common footing with someone. After the struggles of the Fives come the Sixes, which are cooperation cards. They are the first step in moving forward after the conflict of the Fives. Next, Sevens are all about contemplation, reflection, and taking a review of your status. Eights are cards of accomplishment and mastery over a skill and are therefore followed by the Nines, which are completion cards. Tens are transformation cards, as they follow the mastery of a task, emotion, or relationship and therefore represent the beginning of something new.

The Court Cards

The court cards also have universal messages with different intentions. The Pages signify growth and potential. The Knights are messengers and adventurers and are therefore a call for movement and an invitation to start something new. The Queens are mature feminine figures. They each excel at the elements of their respective suit, whether it's the emotional maturity of the Queen of Cups or the independent stability of the Queen of Swords. They are fertile, warm, and motherly. The Kings are the most masterful court cards of their respective suits. They are masculine, well-established, and strong leaders. They have nowhere else to go but to excel into the Major Arcana. Pulling a King upright (more on the meanings of upright and reversed later in this chapter) means that you have progressed, matured, and accomplished a great deal. That work will now unfold in a new, more significant chapter of your life.

Remember that the Minor Arcana are the baby steps in life, and while you can celebrate the victories they represent, they are smaller movements toward the larger goals and achievements of the Major Arcana.

The Major Arcana

The Major Arcana signify important changes or events in the past, present, and future. If you have several of them in a reading, your guides are telling you that you can expect large-scale changes or opportunities. While some of these messages may seem very similar to those of the Minor Arcana, the magnitude of the importance of these cards is much larger.

Number-wise, the Major Arcana start at zero, which is The Fool card. It is a blank slate and a fresh start that, unlike the Aces of the Minor Arcana, has the full knowledge of each of the Minor Arcana cards as it begins its journey. The knowledge and depth of the cards expand with the numbers of the Major Arcana, which go up to twenty-one: The World. Completing the Major Arcana, The World represents all the suits of the deck and the elements of the planet. It is earth, air, fire, and water. It is therefore also Pentacles, Swords, Wands, and Cups—the suits of the Minor Arcana. The World is the culmination of harmony, balance, love, and light. It is both life and death. It is true growth, a fully reached potential. If you pull this card upright in your reading, it is a positive sign for your past, present, or future. Your guides are proud of you, and you should be proud too.

Of course, it isn't just The World that signifies good things: Many of the Major Arcana cards bring positive messages of growth as well as past, present, and future success. The Empress is a positive card when upright, as it represents maturity, a mastery of emotions and finances, strong sexuality, and fertility. This is a card of completed, healthy growth that was well earned. Some of the Major Arcana cards demand action, like The Tower, which points out that your current state is not sustainable and needs to be moved away from.

The most negative of all the Major Arcana cards is The Devil (not Death, as some believe). The Devil is about addiction and temptation, a toxic relationship that is pulling you down. It's a card that reflects getting drawn into something negative and finding escape difficult. The Devil is truly a challenge to overcome. Death, on the other hand, is all about starting a new life or phase of life. Like the snake sheds its skin, the Death card challenges you to shed a former habit, lifestyle, relationship, job—anything that is no longer serving you or is simply something you've outgrown.

TAROT AND THE ZODIAC

The tarot deck is closely aligned with the zodiac. The elements of the Minor Arcana suits correspond to the elements of astrology, and each zodiac sign is therefore linked to a certain tarot suit. All fire astrology signs for example, are linked with the Wands suit. Additionally, each Major Arcana card connects to a specific sign, based on the meaningful life changes and themes encompassed in that card and the correlating traits and possible obstacles of a certain zodiac sign.

It is important to take into consideration the traits of the zodiac involved in the card you pull and whether or not someone with that sign is involved in your question or answer. The following sections outline the traits of the different astrological signs and which tarot cards they most closely align with.

But before diving into the specifics, there are a few helpful terms to know when it comes to understanding the zodiac signs. First are the cardinal, mutable, and fixed aspects of astrology. Cardinal signs (Aries, Cancer, Libra, and Capricorn) occur during the start of a season; as such, they are born leaders. Mutable signs (Gemini, Virgo, Sagittarius, and Pisces) occur in the middle of a season and are therefore flexible—open to change and, overall, comfortable and accepting of it. Fixed signs (Taurus, Leo, Scorpio, and Aquarius) tend to be more stubborn. Occurring at the end of a season, they resist change and would rather put down roots than wander.

Other terms to know are the elements: fire, earth, water, and air. Fire signs (Aries, Leo, and Sagittarius) are passionate and creative. Earth signs (Taurus, Virgo, and Capricorn) are hardworking and dependable. Water signs (Cancer, Scorpio, and Pisces) are emotional and intuitive. And air signs (Gemini, Libra, and Aquarius) are communicative and inventive.

Aries (March 21–April 19)

The astrological calendar begins with a fire sign: Aries. Aries is represented by the ram and is a driving force of ambition, movement, and prosperity. Ariens are creative people who love to leave their mark on the world. They are natural leaders and passionate lovers. The keyword for this sign is most definitely "ambition." Trying to stop an Aries is as successful as standing in the way of a ram. Aries is associated with the Wands suit of the Minor Arcana and The Emperor of the Major Arcana.

Taurus (April 20–May 20)

Taurus is the fixed sign of the earth zodiac, which makes people born under this sign extremely stubborn and resistant to change. This sign is represented appropriately by a bull. Taureans are practical people of action and planning. They are reliable, strong, and grounded and tend to like extravagant things. Like a bull, Taureans can be prone to anger. And their bark *is* as bad as their bite: When this bull is angry, it's best to stay out of the way. Taurus is associated with the Pentacles suit of the Minor Arcana and The Hierophant of the Major Arcana.

Gemini (May 21–June 20)

Gemini is the sign of duality, represented by the twins: two individuals who seem similar but are unique in their goals and desires. Gemini is an air sign, which means they tend to be excellent communicators of various mediums. They are mutable, so they are extremely adaptable; however, this quality combined with their duality can make them abandon tasks easily without finishing them. Gemini is associated with the Swords suit of the Minor Arcana and The Lovers of the Major Arcana.

Cancer (June 21–July 22)

Cancer is a water sign and is represented by the crab. The crab is a bottom dweller of the ocean that is adaptable enough to also survive on land—this adaptability is symbolic of Cancers. They are warm people who excel at making others feel special and loved. The keyword for Cancers is "nurturer." Cancers are also excellent businesspeople and do well in financial careers. Being a water sign, Cancers are very in tune with their emotions, but this can make them extra-sensitive. They are easily offended and can often be broody because of that. They also tend to avoid confrontation. Cancer is associated with the Cups suit of the Minor Arcana and The Chariot of the Major Arcana.

Leo (July 23–August 22)

Leo is the fixed fire sign. Represented by the lion, Leos are ambitious and, like Ariens, want to be remembered. They are artistic and fashionable and have the ability to keep the people around them entertained. Leos, ruled by the Sun, are all about shining bright—and they do, but they are also very generous, loyal, and kind. Leo is associated with the Wands suit of the Minor Arcana and Strength of the Major Arcana.

Virgo (August 23–September 22)

Virgo is the sign of service. Represented by the maiden, this is a sign of purity and good intentions. It is a mutable earth sign, rooted in the realities of life and accepting the changes of life as they come. Virgos like to do good for others and prepare themselves well for the challenges that may lie ahead. They are clear and concise and leave no room for interpretation. Virgo is associated with the Pentacles suit of the Minor Arcana and The Hermit of the Major Arcana.

Libra (September 23–October 22)

Libra is an air sign, represented by the scales of justice. Libras are all about balance, compromise, and bringing harmony to life. They are the peacemakers of the zodiac, and they not only try to settle disputes; they also bring joy wherever they go. They are like Virgos in that they are direct, and they are charming and friendly as well. Libras make friends wherever they are. Libra is associated with the Swords suit of the Minor Arcana and Justice of the Major Arcana.

Scorpio (October 23–November 21)

Scorpio is the fixed water sign of the zodiac. Unlike the other water signs, their water is depicted as frozen, which illustrates that they are resistant to change. But ice also symbolizes a saying that is very true of Scorpio: Still waters run deep. There is a lot going on under the surface of this sign. Represented by the scorpion, Scorpios are excellent listeners and quiet participants in life. They do not do anything without forethought and are always paying attention, taking in all the information possible before acting. Their quiet demeanor makes them secretive, and they can easily be deceitful. They are charming when they want to be but are quick to feel resentment. Scorpio is associated with the Cups suit of the Minor Arcana and Death of the Major Arcana.

Sagittarius (November 22–December 21)

Sagittarius is a fire sign, represented by the archer. It is about pursuing one's personal direction just as the archer pursues their target. Sagittarians are about complete and total honesty with themselves and others; like the archer, they are straight shooters. They love learning and the pursuit of knowledge and are highly intelligent. Because of their ability to see clearly, they are very discerning; Sagittarians don't go where they don't want to go. Sagittarius is associated with the Wands suit of the Minor Arcana and Temperance of the Major Arcana.

Capricorn (December 22–January 19)

Capricorn is an earth sign that enjoys stability and rationality. Capricorns cut right to the point and don't like to waste time or energy on endeavors they deem unworthy, which can make them appear dismissive. Capricorn is represented by the mythical sea-goat. Like the crab of Cancer, the sea-goat is a master of the water and the land, thriving on the stability of mountains to climb with its front feet and using the strength of its seahorse-like tail to propel it through the water. Like the sea goat, Capricorns flourish with structure and reliability and are also reflective and thoughtful. This sign is more complicated than it appears to be, and while Capricorns may have typical nine-to-five jobs, they also support and enjoy the arts. Capricorn is associated with the Pentacles suit of the Minor Arcana and The Devil of the Major Arcana.

Aquarius (January 20–February 18)

Aquarius is an air sign and also the last of the fixed signs. These are creative and innovative people who are happiest when left alone to walk their own paths. Despite being an air sign, Aquarius is represented by the water bearer. The water bearer symbolizes messages from the universe: messages that are carried by the wind and poured onto the earth to cleanse, inspire, and rejuvenate. Aquarians are empathetic people who are devoted to charity. Being so intuitive and empathetic, they are often able to see into the future and are referred to as being "ahead of trends" for that reason. Aquarius is associated with the Swords suit of the Minor Arcana and The Star of the Major Arcana.

Pisces (February 19–March 20)

The year is completed with this deep and dreamy water sign. Pisces tend to be old souls, meaning they have lived many lives before this one. They are often psychic and highly intuitive, even more so than Aquarians. Pisces are represented by two fish, symbolizing the depths of the subconscious that they thrive in. Pisces want to be shut away from the world to be their creative, dreamy, artistic, and empathetic selves. Pisces is associated with the Cups suit of the Minor Arcana and The Moon of the Major Arcana.

CHOOSING YOUR TAROT DECK

Tarot has been practiced for hundreds of years, and many artists have made their own decks with their own vision of what the cards should look like. This makes the tarot world all the more exciting, with room to find the deck that speaks to you. While many people say that purchasing your own tarot deck is bad luck, this is not a universal truth. Like many things in life, the right tarot deck will speak to you, and you should absolutely purchase that deck when you feel the draw. The drinks in Part 2 have been crafted to accompany any tarot deck you choose.

PREPARING FOR A TAROT READING

Tarot reading involves more than just laying out cards. You must prepare your mind, your energy, your deck, and your space before you begin a reading. The following sections explore how to do this preparation to ensure not only that your readings are accurate but also that you are protected from negative entities and guided by the proper spirits.

Setting Up Your Space

It's important to have your space set up properly before you do any of your tarot readings. If your space doesn't have enough room for your cards, stopping to adjust the layout will distract you from the reading and remove your focus. The point is to have your space ready to go, so there are no distractions once you're performing your reading. Start with a clean space with plenty of room to lay out your cards, especially if you're performing a larger spread.

Perform a Spiritual Cleanse

You need to spiritually cleanse the space along with literally cleaning it. Cleansing your space spiritually removes negative entities that may be hanging around, looking for an opening to cling to you and feed on your energy. Remember that when you perform a tarot reading, you are opening a portal for your guides to enter and give you messages. Through that portal, a negative entity may also enter. Remove the risk by cleansing your space of negative entities before you open yourself up.

To cleanse the space spiritually, open a window and cleanse your space by lighting a chosen herb or incense and moving around the space with the herb or incense so that the smoke reaches every inch of the area. Some herbs are stronger than others, so if you feel a particularly heavy energy in your space, you should use a stronger cleansing herb. Palo santo, which is a kind of wood rather than an herb, is one of the strongest types of cleansing materials and is appropriate for monthly maintenance of your tarot space. Performing weekly cleanses with sage is good for general upkeep in between palo santo cleanses.

Make sure that, in addition to the surface and card deck you're working with, you also cleanse the corners of the room and behind any appliances or furniture like a television, couch, or refrigerator. Make sure that you do a smoke cleanse around any knick-knacks, paintings, or photographs with faces as well. The dead or dormant spaces behind appliances are areas where negative entities tend to hang, and anything with a face attracts entities to attach to it. As you move around the room and cleanse the space, repeat, "If you have any negative intentions, you are not welcome here." Cleansing like this weekly, whether you're doing a reading or not, is good for keeping your space spiritually clean. If you perform this weekly, doing a less thorough cleanse and focusing only on the deck and your immediate reading space is sufficient.

Invite Your Spirit Guides

With the window still open, begin a smoke cleanse with an herb or incense that attracts spirits (cedar and frankincense work well). As you perform your smoke cleanse, repeat, "If you have positive intentions, you are welcome here" and call to your spirit guides specifically, welcoming them into your space. Your spirit guides will help guide your reading and aid your intuition as you decipher the meaning of the cards. Often, the spirits you are summoning are ancestors. Once you are done summoning your guides, feel free to close the window.

Once your space has been cleansed and your guides have been welcomed, fill a glass of water. Holding it in your right hand, tell the water that you need it to act as a conduit for spirits to communicate with you. Place it on your tarot workspace (out of the way of where your card spread will go, of course). Then, hold an unscented candle in your right hand and ask it to also be a conduit for spirits to use. Light the candle and place it on or near your workspace. These two items will help provide your spirit guides with the energy to communicate with you.

Protecting Your Energy

Before you do a reading, especially if it's for someone other than yourself, it's important to create an energy shield around yourself to protect your own energy. Doing this keeps your energy from being drained by the reading, but it also protects you from negative entities attaching to you. Energy shields can feel difficult to create at first, but the more you do this practice, the easier it becomes.

Begin creating your shield by closing your eyes and doing some deep breathing, clearing your mind from the stresses of your day. Then, visualize a colored light encompassing your whole body; the color completely surrounds you in a protective glow. Black is a good color to visualize, as it deters negative energy, but as long as you believe the color you see will protect you, that's all that matters. If you can create layers of colors, that's useful because the layers offer more protection, like layers of warm clothes on a cold day.

This is a great technique to do daily, regardless of whether you're performing a reading, as it protects your energy from all outside influences and any negative entities that might attach to you.

It's important to keep in mind that the practice of reading tarot takes a lot of energy, so doing many readings in one day will thoroughly drain you. Being energetically drained will also impact the accuracy of your readings. Doing shorter readings for yourself is a good place to start when you're a beginner. Starting your days with a short cleanse and a one-card draw is a great way to learn and become more in tune with your spirit guides. Helping friends with readings is another great way to grow your intuition. Just make sure you don't stretch yourself too thin.

COMPLETING A TAROT READING

Now that you know how to protect yourself, cleanse your space, and welcome in your guides, let's explore the details of doing a tarot reading, from cleansing your deck, to drawing and interpreting your card.

Cleanse the Deck

To begin a reading, you must first cleanse your deck. One effective way to do this is by closing your eyes and holding the deck in your right hand. (Your right side is your projective, or dominant, side, and using your right hand puts your energy into the object you are holding.) Next, visualize the energy of the moon coming down from the universe and traveling to you. The light meets the top of your skull and is now inside your head. Continue to visualize that light traveling through your brain, down your neck, your right shoulder and arm, and into your hand. Visualize the light encapsulating your tarot deck. You may feel your arm shudder before releasing the cards. Knock three times on your deck.

Some people simply knock three times on their deck between uses. Others may cleanse their deck by burning different kinds of incense, dried herbs, or wood with ancient, holy cleansing abilities. You can do this by lighting your chosen herb, wood, or incense, holding your deck in your right hand, and holding the cleansing agent in your left. Use the smoke to wrap around your deck. Tell the deck that you rid it of all negative energy that might be within or around it. It is best to try a few different methods of cleansing your deck to see what feels right and what works best for you.

Shuffle the Deck

When you shuffle your deck, do so in a way that is most comfortable for you. You can vary your shuffle style to ensure you're not just mixing up the cards but you're also getting your energy on the deck. Close your eyes and ask your guides what you need from them for guidance as you shuffle. You can focus on a specific question if you have one; just make sure you avoid yes or no questions, as there isn't a yes or no card in tarot. Your cards are there to show you the way and illuminate your problem and your path. You can also just ask what your day looks like or what type of energy you need to thrive on a particular day. You can ask small or big questions: it's all about what you need in that moment. You can try visualizing the object of your question if that is applicable. You can even repeat your question out loud as you shuffle.

Next, put the deck down with your right hand and, also with your right hand, cut the deck into three piles, then restack them into one pile in any order that feels right to you. That feeling is your growing intuition as you trust your spirit guides to literally guide you.

Draw Your Cards

Now begin drawing cards for whichever spread you've chosen, from the top of the deck you've just stacked. In the case of this book, you will only be drawing one card, unless you want multiple cocktails. Don't forget to cleanse your deck between readings, even if they are all for the same person.

DIFFERENT SPREADS

There is no shortage of spread options for tarot readings. The following are the more popular spreads.

Celtic Cross

Perhaps the most popular and frequently used spread is the Celtic Cross. This involves ten cards that you arrange starting with one card in the middle, then crossing the next card on top of the first. You pull your third card just below the first two, the fourth to the left of the center, the fifth directly above the initial two cards, and the sixth to the right of them. Then, you pull the final four cards from the bottom to top, lining them up to the right of the cross you made with the previous cards.

The first card pulled in this spread is the present heart of the matter or the focus of the reading. The second is what stands in your way (which is why this card literally crosses and lies on top of the first card). The third is the root of your situation, the fourth is your past, and the fifth is the overall goal. The sixth card you pull is the future based on all the cards that fell before it. The seventh represents you, and the eighth represents your external influences. The ninth card shows your hopes and fears, and, finally, the tenth card is the projected outcome based on all the cards that fell before it.

Three-Card Spread

Another common spread is the simple three-card pull from left to right for the past, present, and future. This is a fast and easy way to get a feel for a specific and small question. This reading might help you decide whether or not you want to proceed with a relationship or apply for a job. You can count on this reading to point out your past behavior, how that's affected your present, and how it could affect your future. Remember that any card that lands in the future placement of your spread is liable to change depending on your present actions.

Nine-Card Spread

Extending the three-card past, present, and future concept to a nine-card pull is another useful spread. Start your rows from left to right, but create three rows of three cards. Three cards tell a story of the past, three cards of the present, and three cards of the future. Starting with a three-card spread and expanding to a nine-card spread is a great way to hone your skill in tarot. But this nine-card spread is also a go-to for many seasoned and skilled readers. Unlike the three-card roots of this spread, this nine-card spread is a great way to look at your current, past, and future journey because when you pull three times as many cards, you get three times as much information. Patterns will often show themselves in this spread. Even a break in patterns may show up, and that's always nice to see because it shows even further personal growth. It's like putting the three-card spread under a microscope.

New Year's Wheel

Another simple spread is a New Year's Wheel. This spread includes a card for each month, placed in a circle. Each card represents a theme for the given month. Place the cards clockwise starting at twelve o'clock and move around the clock. After completing the circle, place the thirteenth card in the middle. This card represents the overall theme of your upcoming year. This wheel is also a great spread to use for birthdays.

Seven-Day Spread

Not unlike the New Year's Wheel spread is the seven-day spread. This spread is an overview of what each of your days and the forthcoming week will be like. Note that the first card you pull will be for the following day. So if you are doing your reading for the week on a Tuesday, the first card you pull will refer to Wednesday. Do not worry about doing a seven-day spread on a certain day of the week: Your guides don't adhere to a Monday–Friday workweek like people do. However, Mondays are great days to do any type of reading because they are the Moon's Day and the day of the week when spirits are most active in our world.

Expanding a Spread

It's important to note that if you do a short spread and feel your question hasn't been answered, it's okay to pull another card (or a few more cards) to clarify the answer. However, this isn't necessary with spreads like the Celtic Cross, which are more focused than the broader three-card past, present, and future spread. Using a pendulum to clarify a question with a yes or no answer is also helpful when working to understand a tarot reading.

It is also entirely possible for you to create your own spread. In fact, as you grow your intuition, designing your own spread can be beneficial in developing your relationship to the cards, as well as your ever-growing relationship with your spirit guides.

REVERSED CARDS

Pulling a card upside down (reversed) is an important consideration when interpreting your reading. Reversed cards indicate a blockage in the energy that the card typically projects when upright. Its meaning can be very close to the opposite of the upright card, but it can also indicate more of a disconnect than the exact opposite meaning. Pulling a card reversed may also be a call to put in a certain kind of work so that you may reap the benefits of the positive elements of the card. Seeing a reversed card in your future makes that action achievable, and pulling it in your present represents an opportunity to change, though it must be immediate. Nothing is set in stone when it comes to the present and the future; the cards and your spirit guides are just pointing out the path that you are currently on. If you want to veer from that path, you must put in the work. Your spirit guides are happy to point out where to work, how hard the work will be, and what the result will be.

Outsourcing a Reading

When doing a reading for yourself concerning a highly emotional subject during a high-tension time, it's very possible that your emotions will cloud your energy and judgment. Not only can your energy draw you to certain cards; your interpretation of the cards can be clouded as well. You may unknowingly ignore your spirit guides to interpret the reading in a way that is favorable to your desired outcome, not the reality. For that reason, it is sometimes best to outsource a tarot reading and ask a friend or professional to read for you. Not only is it nice to support a talented person; having an outside reflection on your situation is also enormously beneficial.

POST-READING RITUALS

After your reading is complete, take a moment to yourself and cleanse the energy of the reading. Close your eyes and take three long, deep breaths. Release any stress or negative energy that may have come from the reading. Visualize the glowing light around you once more, ensuring that no breaks in the light have happened when you were focused on the reading. Breaks allow for something to get in or out, just like water leaking from a cracked glass. Take a moment to thank your spirit guides for their help and insight, and don't forget to cleanse your deck with your preferred method.

When you extinguish the candle you lit during preparations for the reading, be sure to snuff it out rather than blow it out. Blowing out candles with your intentions in them will blow your intentions away with the flame. This candle now has the intentions you set in it, and every time you light the wick, the candle will serve as an energy source for spirits to guide you. So don't use this candle for ambiance: This is your tarot reading candle only.

Discard the water you poured before the reading and thank your spirit guides again for their help and guidance.

Open a window and smoke cleanse your space once more, removing the energy of your reading.

CONTINUING YOUR TAROT JOURNEY

Now that you've learned how to cleanse and protect your energy and perform a few different styles of readings, it's time to start drawing cards and creating your inspired drinks...almost. First, you will want to take a look at the basics of bartending in the next chapter. Remember that just as you work to grow your psychic intuition, you can also grow your bartending skills, and an understanding of the main tools and techniques is a wonderful place to start.

CHAPTER 2

BARTENDING BASICS

Like tarot reading, bartending is a lot about intuition and trust. You need to trust yourself to be able to put flavors and textures together, as much as you need to trust yourself to interpret the meaning of a tarot card appearing in your spread. As with tarot, the more you practice bartending, the better you become. And just like having the right tarot deck and all the tools to cleanse and prepare your space for your readings, having the proper tools on your bar and understanding key terms in mixing cocktails will allow you to make the most of the bartending experience.

In this chapter, you will discover what equipment you should have on hand for creating the drinks in Part 2. You will also learn the differences between shaking and stirring a cocktail (and why they matter), measurement terms you will encounter in drink recipes, how to flame an orange swath, and what glassware is used for different types of drinks. Use this chapter to cultivate your personal tarot bar kit.

NECESSITIES FOR THE TAROT READER'S BAR

Before you start making the cocktails in this book, you will want to have a few helpful tools on hand. Prepare your home tarot bar with the following.

Barspoon

A barspoon with a long handle and sleek bowl is an integral part of stirring your cocktails. If you don't have the proper spoon and stir, you could easily overdilute or aerate the cocktail; you could even bruise the cocktail (more common in overly shaken drinks, bruising is the result of dilution and oxygen in a drink, making it murky with floating ice chips). Slim spoons or teardrop spoons are easy to work with because when the bowl of the spoon is too big, it creates more room for mistakes. A slimmer bowl means less chance for error. Some barspoons don't have an actual bowl at all, just two teardrops (one on either end of the spoon). If you get one of these, however, also getting one with an actual bowl is imperative for many measurements.

Cocktail Shaker

The Boston shaker is a tried-and-true cocktail shaker that is simple and affordable and creates the best seal on the market. There are other options, like shakers that have three pieces, but these can leak. There is also the Parisian shaker, which is the same shape as the three-piece shaker, but it has only two pieces. Choose a cocktail shaker that has two metal pieces and no glass—even if it's tempered. A Boston shaker full of liquid and ice won't break when it's dropped because it's made of metal and has that solid Boston shaker seal. No one wants to clean up a sticky mess, especially in their own kitchen.

Glassware

Picking out glassware is a fun activity when you're ready to present your creations. It's important to have an "up" or stemmed glass, like a coupe, Nick and Nora, classic Manhattan, or martini glass. Other must-haves are champagne flutes, rocks glasses, and Collins or highball glasses. Tiki glasses are fun to collect, and a lot of secondhand shops have eye-catching vintage options. Having a couple of each type gives you space to have fun when you're mixing at home (and allows you to properly show off your tarot libation in all its divine splendor!).

The recipes in this book use the following types of glasses: rocks, martini, Collins, coupe, classic Manhattan, pint, shot, Nick and Nora, red and white wine, toddy mug, copper mug, and champagne flute, but you can mix things up and choose what works for you and the presentation you want for your creation.

Ice

The tarot recipes call for ice cubes, king cubes, and pebble ice. Ice cubes are standard cubes good for shaking, stirring, and serving drinks on the rocks. King cubes are 4-ounce cubes that are nice to have on hand for at-home stirred drinks. These are also great to use for freezing garnishes. They usually come in cubes, but you can also find them in balls, skulls, diamonds, and other fun shapes. When using a number of cubes in a drink, a silicone ice tray will ensure uniform, dense cubes.

Jigger

The jigger is your measuring tool. There are lots of different styles, and the style you choose is really up to your preference. Some jiggers have a ½ ounce on one side and 1 ounce on the other; others have 1 ounce on one side and 2 ounces on the other. There are even jiggers that look like tiny measuring cups with multiple measurements inside. It is best to pick one that gives as many measurements as possible. Many have notches inside to indicate a ½- or ¾-ounce measurement. Jiggers with no notches or lines for smaller amounts limit your ability to accurately measure smaller amounts—making it more difficult to create consistent or precise cocktails.

Mixing Glass

The first thing a bartender learns is when to shake and when to stir a cocktail. A cocktail is always shaken if it contains a citrus or juice to ensure all ingredients are mixed thoroughly. If it's entirely alcohol, it must be stirred. Therefore, you need a mixing glass. You can get really fancy with your mixing glass and buy something handmade, hand-blown, or crystal. You can also get a tempered glass that looks like a pint glass (or 16-ounce glass) or larger, which tends to be less expensive.

Don't bother getting a glass with measurements etched or printed on it; it's better to use a jigger to measure ingredients before you start pouring them into your mixing glass. You will want to fill the glass halfway with ice unless a recipe specifies otherwise.

Muddler

Muddlers are for more than just mojitos! They are a simple but necessary tool for anyone who enjoys a cocktail with fresh fruit and herbs. With a muddler, you can easily throw berries into a classic cocktail to spice it up with something fresh and different. In this book, you will need a muddler for Blueberry Syrup (Chapter 3) and The Magician's Creation (Chapter 8).

While muddlers were often traditionally made of wood, today's muddlers are made with other materials. Wood is porous and expands, which means it tends to split because it responds to changing temperatures, and attracts mold from the trapped moisture and particles of fruit, sugar, and herbs. Of course, metal muddlers can easily crack glass, even tempered glass. For that reason, it's best not to muddle in your mixing glass or any glass, no matter what type of muddler you have. Keep your berries or citrus in one half of your shaker when you muddle to prevent a mess and potential injury.

Plastic muddlers are generally considered to be the best. Plastic is easy to clean and, like wood muddlers, it is lighter in weight and just as effective. Plastic muddlers are also inexpensive.

Strainers

You will need a Hawthorne strainer for your shaken drinks. This fits nicely in a cocktail shaker, so you can easily strain your cocktail into a glass. The best option is the simplest: one without a long handle, which just becomes cumbersome and is unnecessary. The best Hawthorne strainer has a notch to place your finger for balance. This will give you more control when you pour your cocktail.

A tea strainer is also great to have, but it is not entirely necessary for the average home bartender. You will want one to make the Dreaming While Awake cocktail in this book. It is used to double-strain shaken drinks, so you would use it with your Hawthorne strainer. To double-strain a drink, pour from the shaker through the Hawthorne strainer while holding the tea strainer under the liquid being poured before the drink reaches the glass. Many bartenders double-strain all their shaken cocktails to catch any ice chips and prevent unwanted dilution. A tea strainer is made with fine mesh and is great for drinks with muddled fruit or herbs—anything that you don't want to get caught in your teeth while you're enjoying that divinely inspired cocktail. Tea strainers are also helpful for double-straining drinks that include egg whites (like in the Dreaming While Awake). A home bartender should consider this style of strainer a preference, not a necessity.

A julep cocktail strainer is ideal for straining stirred drinks from your mixing glass into your drinking glass. Like the Hawthorne strainer, a julep cocktail strainer with a notch for your finger will add balance as you strain. Pouring a cocktail with one hand can be difficult, especially when a glass filled with ice and liquid is involved, so having added support is recommended.

BARTENDING TERMS AND TECHNIQUES

Along with the different tools, there are key terms and techniques you will encounter and use to make the drinks in this book. Believe it or not, there is a right way and a wrong way to stir or shake a drink. There is also a very fun trick to learn that will make you look like a magician and add a gorgeous bouquet to your cocktail!

How to Measure a Dash and a Pinch

Your jigger gives you everything from $1/8$ ounce and up, but what if you want an even smaller amount, such as for those ingredients with a highly concentrated flavor? This is why you will see the terms "dash" and "pinch" in this book and other cocktail books and recipes.

The vessel your liquid is contained in will usually have a top that allows you to get a single dash (also sometimes called a "splash") out of the container at a time, because those things, like bitters and orange blossom water, are meant to be added to a drink in small portions due to their strong flavors. Simply hold the container upside down over your cocktail shaker, mixing glass, or cocktail glass, and give it a slight jerk (or light squeeze, if using a plastic bottle) for each dash the recipe calls for. If you're working with fresh juice this might be trickier because you won't have it in a plastic bottle to lightly squeeze. In these instances, you can use your barspoon! Barspoons are for more than stirring: They're also a unique unit of cocktail measurements. About one-fourth of the barspoon is equal to a dash. Don't overthink the exact measurement—it isn't intended to be precise.

And don't overthink it when measuring out a "pinch" either. Simply pour a small amount of the salt or spice you are using into the palm of your hand, take a pinch of it with your other hand, and add it to your drink.

How to Stir and Shake a Drink

Every cocktail recipe has an unwritten ingredient: water. Every single drink (both in this book or beyond) is intended to incorporate half an ounce of water whether shaken or stirred. This is why the shaking and stirring processes are so important. This also means that your ice shape and quality affect the drink as well. Thinner ice that is easier to break down will mean that you need shorter shakes and stirs to blend the ingredients.

As mentioned previously, drinks made up of only alcohols will be stirred, while drinks with other ingredients like citrus or juice will be shaken. When you stir your drink, first put ice in your mixing glass (enough to fill it halfway) and then add the remaining ingredients. Place the spoon between the ice and the glass and stir, using the momentum of the ice to guide your spoon as you begin to stir slightly faster. A stir should only last about 30–45 seconds. More stirring can water down the cocktail, and less stirring will make it under-diluted.

For a shaken drink, you build your cocktail with ice in the cocktail shaker, seal the shaker, and shake for about half the time you stir (about 15–20 seconds). The reason you shake for less time is that the ice breaks up and therefore melts faster when being shaken than when it is stirred. Again, you don't want to over-dilute.

If you are working with an egg white or flip (a flip is a cocktail with an entire egg or just the yolk in it), the shaking process is a little different. First, you want to dry shake, which means shaking your cocktail with no ice. If you are just getting started bartending, you can add a cube of ice to act as a timer for this step. Shake until you can't hear the cube, then stop, add the remaining ice, and shake for about 2 more minutes. This will create a great, thick, frothy head for your cocktail. Once you get used to the timing, you can stop using the single cube as a timer. Dry shaking is also great for cocktails that are served on crushed or pebble ice, because these types of ice dilute a lot faster than standard cubes. You will also see the term "dirty rocks" in some of the recipes in this book and elsewhere in the cocktail world. This term simply means to pour all the rocks you've shaken with, into the glass with the cocktail rather than straining it over fresh ice.

How to Flame an Orange Swath

You may have seen bartenders flaming orange swaths (large peels) over your drinks. This is a skill that every bartender should be able to learn, and it isn't difficult—but it is fun. You'll find recipes that use orange and lemon swaths, including Stand Your Ground (Chapter 4).

First, you need a match and an orange swath. Make sure you have a good-sized swath that is juicy and not too thin. The pith should be a part of the swath. A soft orange will be riper and easier to peel, and it will have a good amount of oil that makes it easier to set on fire.

Next, light your match and let it burn a little, holding the match horizontally to get a strong flame. Then, holding your orange swath in the other hand, rotate the swath over the flame to dry it slightly before expressing it. Expressing a swath means squeezing it, skin-side out, over your cocktail so that the oils are released. (The pith has no oils.) This gives cocktails a nice, citrusy bouquet. In the case of flaming a swath, you are expressing the oils by squeezing the peel over the flame. Practice this over the sink a few times to get the hang of it.

SPIRITS

You may know the terms for different spirits, but it's important to understand what they are and what flavors they bring to a cocktail. This will make you more informed as a home bartender and give you the confidence and ability to make substitutions and create your own recipes. Like tarot, the more cocktail building knowledge you have, the more fun and success you get from the process. And, like tarot reading, the more bartending skills you acquire, the more fun you will have sharing them with your friends and family.

Vodka

Vodka is a spirit distilled from a starch. It can be made from a grain, sugar beets, or potatoes. Vodka is often called the "flavorless" spirit, and while that's not necessarily true (everything has a flavor), it does have very light flavors that blend well and make it easy to mix with. However, that doesn't mean you can substitute vodka for the base spirit of any cocktail and get the same result. Replacing the rum in a mojito with vodka, for example, won't create a similar cocktail because the vodka won't bring any of the rich and rounded sweet, vanilla notes a rum does to the drink. It won't make the drink taste bad, but it will make it very different.

Gin

Gin is a grain alcohol that consists of 70 percent or more juniper (anything less would be considered vodka). Other ingredients in gin are filtered water and a variety of botanicals. Because of that 30 percent of botanicals, gin comes in a lot of different flavors, which can make shopping for the right one a fun challenge. Feel free to experiment with different types. Each one is a little different and brings its own flavor to whatever cocktail it is added to. Hendrick's Gin, for example, is distilled with cucumbers and rose petals, which gives it a distinct flavor. The Queen's Mirror recipe in Chapter 5 calls for a London dry–style gin, which is a common style to use. London dry gins tend to be juniper-forward, citrusy, and with hints of pine. Try something new or use the brand you usually enjoy.

Rum

Rum is made with cane sugar, molasses, and/or evaporated cane sugar. Rum can be aged in a variety of barrels or spiced, which just means more flavors are added. Just because a rum is white (also called "silver" or "light") does not mean it is less flavorful than one that is spiced or aged (also called "dark"). White rum has a wonderful array of sweet, tropical, candy flavors, among others. Because rum is easy to make, it is distilled all over the world, though some of the ingredients are sourced from specific countries. Many distilleries make the most of the features of their surrounding environment to create traditional, high-quality rums.

Mezcal

Mezcal is a distilled spirit that can be made from any species of agave. It is roasted in the ground in various creative manners either on its own or with ingredients like fruit, rabbit, or ham, to name a few. Mezcal is generally recognized for being a smoky tequila, but not all mezcals are smoky. The agave plants used in specific mezcals offer a wonderful array of flavors, and if they are roasted with additional items like rabbit or fruit, those notes infuse into the flavor of the product. The world of mezcal is huge and delicious.

Tequila

Tequila is a category of mezcal. It must be distilled from the Weber Azul agave plant, a specific cultivar of *Agave tequilana*, to be categorized as a tequila. Blanco, reposado, and añejo tequilas all come from that same agave plant. The difference between these three tequilas is in how long they have been aged. Blanco tequila has not been aged, which is why it retains the clear color of a distilled spirit. Reposado tequila has been aged between two and twelve months in oak barrels, which gives it a brown tint, like whiskey. Añejo tequila has been aged at least one year and up to three years, also in oak barrels. Extra añejo tequila also exists, which entails aging tequila even longer.

Whiskey

Whiskey is a grain spirit. Just like you wouldn't order "a wine" from a bar, you wouldn't order "a whiskey." Just as you would say "a dry red wine" or "a Grüner" when ordering your wine, you will have to be specific when ordering whiskey. Popular varieties are bourbons, ryes, Irish whiskey, scotch, and Japanese whiskey. All whiskeys have specific requirements for their categorization.

Bourbon

Bourbon is an American invention, produced by immigrants who wanted to re-create the whiskeys from their home countries. It is made with 51 percent or more corn and aged at least two years in virgin American oak barrels. The composition of the remaining 49 percent varies, which is one detail that makes each bourbon exciting to try. Many bourbons are blends of various barrels, which are mixed for the best taste. If the bourbon is from one barrel, the bottle will note "single barrel" on its label. Flavor-wise, bourbons tend to be a little bit sweeter and softer than ryes.

Rye

Rye is a whiskey made with 51 percent or more rye grain. It is generally a little spicier than bourbon for that reason. Like bourbon, the ingredients composing the remaining 49 percent can vary. Rye must be aged at least two years in charred, new oak barrels.

Irish Whiskey

Irish whiskey is exactly what it sounds like: a whiskey made in Ireland. It is a blend of three different whiskeys: triple-distilled pot-stilled malt whiskey, pot-stilled unmalted barley whiskey, and column-stilled grain whiskey. Irish whiskey is also aged, often in Spanish sherry casks or used American oak barrels, and while the style of barrel does not matter, they must be aged for at least three years

Scotch

Scotch is a whiskey made in Scotland and is best known for its peaty flavor. There are four regions in Scotland that produce scotch: the Highlands, Speyside, the Lowlands, and Islay. Each region creates unique flavor profiles depending on its environment and proximity to the sea. All types must be aged in oak barrels for at least three years, and many are several scotches blended together to make an "older" scotch.

Japanese Whiskey

A Japanese whiskey must be produced in Japan, even if the bulk of the ingredients are not. The grain, peat, and barley are all largely sourced from Scotland, but Japanese distillers often use their iconic clear, mineral-rich water for scotch distillation. Age-wise, the process varies, though most whiskeys are aged at least three years. Japanese whiskey has been produced since the 1920s in Japan, but it really took America by storm only in more recent years.

SHAKING, STIRRING, AND MUDDLING TAROT MAGIC

Once you have all your bartending tools, spirits, and techniques ready, you can start mixing at home. But before you begin making the drinks in Part 2, take a look at the next chapter on special additions for your cocktails. These are unique and simple options to imbue your creations with magic, as well as unique flavors.

CHAPTER 3

HOMEMADE SYRUPS AND SPECIAL ADDITIONS

———————◆———————

Homemade syrups and other special drink additions are great for the home bartender and magic practitioner alike. For one thing, they are inexpensive. Homemade syrups also add flavor to nonalcoholic drink options for when you aren't in the mood for alcohol or don't drink it, or if you want to share a mocktail with friends or family. For magic practitioners, mixing with herbs is a natural part of many routines. Herbs have been used for spells, tonics, and medicines for centuries; working with herbs not only infuses your drinks with flavor; it puts a little magic in your concoction as well.

In this chapter, you will discover easy tips and recipes for making the special additions used in Part 2. The recipes provided are featured throughout the remaining chapters of this book because the tarot is so closely linked to flora. Every herb used, whether it's a garnish or infused syrup, is chosen not just for flavor and color but also for its magical properties and uses that correspond with the imagery and messages of the cards. With a few steps, you will be making interesting, versatile, and magical enhancements for your drinks.

MAKING SYRUPS

The following section includes recipes for the syrups used in the cocktails as well as tips and suggestions for creating your own original syrup recipes. Just like with home bartending and learning tarot, this section arms you with knowledge and intuition in progressing beyond these pages. As you re-create the recipes, take note of the techniques and concepts and use them to make your own magical syrups.

Use Outside Knowledge

Don't be afraid to integrate your cooking or baking skills into your syrups. Before you start, think about the flavor you're trying to achieve and consider if you've ever done anything similar in the kitchen. How did you do it? Can you incorporate that process now?

Think of the Syrup Like Tea

The best advice for making a syrup that uses herbs is to "let it steep like tea." Often, you'll just let the herbs or fruit sit and infuse into the sugar, honey, agave, or whatever your sweetening base is. Sometimes that may mean heating it, but if you do that, you run the risk of cooking the herbs and changing their flavor profile, so consider this before you start. You may want to do a cold infusion by mixing the sweetening base and water and allowing the herbs or fruit to sit for a few hours, a day, or longer.

Get Creative

Don't be afraid to make mistakes and get weird. Remember, it's just sugar and herbs, fruit, or vegetables. Try making small batches in different ways so you can compare them. In the same vein, don't be afraid to take someone else's recipe and replace a step or ingredient as you see fit. The worst that can happen is you don't like it and simply start again. The best that can happen is you have a fantastic new syrup to use at your home bar.

Taste Daily

Don't give up on a syrup if it doesn't immediately taste the way you want it to taste. Especially when making a cold infusion, time really matters. Taste your syrup daily, and you will find stronger flavors emerging.

Adjust Ingredients and Steps for Magical Practices

Recipes will look a bit different if you have an intention for their use beyond flavor. If you want your syrup to perform something specific like a love or lust spell, make sure you've chosen the appropriate herb, like lavender, hibiscus, or rose. As you make the syrup, use your right hand to put the herbs into the liquid, tell them what you want them to do for you, thank them for their help, and ask for their favors. Some recipes in this chapter include these steps for infusing magical intent into certain ingredients.

SIMPLE SYRUP

Simple Syrup is as easy to make and mix with as its name promises. It is equal parts sugar and water, and you can easily double this recipe or cut it down. If a recipe calls for a "rich" simple syrup, that just means it has more sugar than water. Every home bartender should always have simple syrup in their refrigerator because it's so versatile and is the glue that holds a lot of cocktails together. It offers texture, sweetness, and roundness, and it mellows out the acidity of citrus.

1. In a small saucepan, heat sugar and water over medium heat, stirring constantly, until sugar is dissolved.
2. Store in a sealed container in refrigerator for up to 2 weeks.

YIELDS 1 CUP

½ cup filtered water

½ cup granulated sugar

CUCUMBER SYRUP

Cucumber Syrup takes the place of muddling cucumber for the classic Pimm's Cup and the Two of Pimm's Cups variation in Chapter 5. This syrup is also good for mocktails and would make a delicious cucumber lemonade. Cucumbers bring inner and outer beauty when used in magic, so having this syrup on hand is just what you need to glow up your inner and outer looks.

1. Place cucumbers in a juicer to extract liquid.
2. Combine cucumber juice and Simple Syrup. Strain excess cucumber pieces.
3. Store in a sealed container in refrigerator for up to 1 week.

YIELDS 1 CUP

2 large cucumbers, peeled

1 cup Simple Syrup (see previous recipe)

CHAMOMILE SYRUP

Chamomile is a flower that has been used to relax and induce sleep for ages. This mystical herb is put in teas to enhance meditation and psychic abilities and to calm the mind. Using this Chamomile Syrup in your cocktails infuses the flavors with the intentions of chamomile: to protect, to relax, to help with intuition and opening of the third eye. This syrup starts with the build of a Simple Syrup recipe by adding just two steeped chamomile tea bags. It functions as hot water would in traditional tea.

YIELDS 1 CUP

½ cup turbinado sugar

½ cup filtered water

2 tea bags chamomile tea, steeped

1. In a small saucepan, heat sugar and water over medium heat, stirring constantly, until sugar is dissolved.

2. Remove from heat, add tea bags, cover, and allow to sit until syrup cools, about 1 hour.

3. Remove tea bags and store in a sealed container in refrigerator for up to 2 weeks.

AGAVE SYRUP

Agave Syrup is another must-have in your home bar. This is an easy way to add body to any cocktail or mocktail. It enriches The Flaming Tower (Chapter 8) better than Simple Syrup because it adds a round, sweet, almost honey-like flavor. You may want to add Agave Syrup to your coffee or tea or use it to replace the sugar in your lemonade. Agave itself is a magical herb that represents fertility, long life, and health. It has been used to heal, protect, and even promote lust.

YIELDS 1 CUP
½ cup agave nectar
½ cup filtered water

1. In a sealable container, combine agave and water and stir until well mixed.
2. Store in a sealed container in refrigerator for up to 2 weeks.

HONEY SYRUP

Honey mixed with milk has been offered to the gods, but that's not all. Honey is featured on a long list of magical properties and spells. It is linked to the goddess Aphrodite and has been used in spell jars to "sweeten" or improve a person's mood for countless years. Honey is also used in spellwork to keep two things together and to promote prosperity and fertility and to cleanse a sacred space.

YIELDS 1 CUP
½ cup amber honey
½ cup filtered water

1. In a sealable container, combine honey and water until cohesive.
2. Store in a sealed container in refrigerator for up to 2 weeks.

Cilantro Syrup

Butterfly Pea Flower Tincture

Honey Syrup

Blueberry Syrup

BLUEBERRY SYRUP

Like Cucumber Syrup, Blueberry Syrup is great to have in your home bar for cocktails and mocktails. It is used in The Emperor's Cerebral Energy recipe in Chapter 8. The base of this syrup is agave rather than sugar, because the fat of the agave pairs better with the blueberries, giving this syrup a nice texture and body. Blueberries are known to improve memory and overall cognitive function, and also contain prebiotics linked to lowered blood sugar.

YIELDS 1 CUP

½ cup agave nectar

½ cup filtered water

½ cup fresh blueberries

1. In a sealable container, combine agave and water and stir until well mixed.

2. Add blueberries to mixture. Slightly muddle to burst blueberries. Do not over-muddle.

3. Cover and allow to sit in refrigerator at least 6 hours up to overnight.

4. Strain, cover, and store in refrigerator for up to 2 weeks.

LAVENDER HONEY SYRUP

Like honey, lavender has been used in spellwork for ages. It is used to promote sleep, to calm, and to help create restfulness. Baby products are often scented with the gentle fragrance of lavender, and so are bath soaks for adults, tinctures, and even household cleaning products. Lavender is used by witches to attract love and lust, particularly lust. This is a great flower and syrup to work with if you want to get pregnant, as it blends the fertility energy of honey with the lust of the lavender.

YIELDS 1 CUP
½ cup amber honey
½ cup filtered water
½ cup dried lavender buds

1. In a small saucepan, heat all ingredients over low heat, and stir until honey and water are well mixed. Allow mixture to boil, then remove from heat and cool about 1 hour.

2. Strain into a sealable container and store in refrigerator for up to 2 weeks.

HIBISCUS SYRUP

This syrup is a less rich, lighter, and less tart option than the Hibiscus Grenadine later in this chapter. For that reason, these two recipes result in vastly different syrups.

YIELDS 1 CUP
½ cup granulated sugar
½ cup filtered water
1 tablespoon dried hibiscus petals

1. In a small saucepan, heat water over medium heat and add sugar. Stir until dissolved.

2. Add hibiscus petals and allow to steep 5 minutes.

3. Strain into a sealable container and store in refrigerator for up to 2 weeks.

CHAI SYRUP

Chai tea is a blend of herbs including cloves, cinnamon, nutmeg, ginger, star anise, and cardamom. Recipes differ, and therefore, so do the herbs used. Many people even make their own chai tea blends. Use the tea brand that you already enjoy or try a new one. Common ingredients like cinnamon and nutmeg draw in money and wealth. Cinnamon is very versatile in spellwork and can protect your household, ensure victory, and even promote lust. Star anise supports clarity and psychic abilities, and ginger offers clairvoyance, stomach-healing properties, and increased self-confidence.

1. In a sealable container, combine sugar and water until sugar is dissolved.
2. Add tea bag and allow to steep 10 minutes before removing. Discard tea bag.
3. Store in a sealed container in refrigerator for up to 2 weeks.

YIELDS ½ CUP

¼ cup granulated sugar

¼ cup filtered hot water

1 chai tea bag

STARFRUIT SYRUP

Starfruit has a very subtle flavor, which is why macerating the fruit before making it into a syrup helps those flavors pop. Macerating is a process whereby you let the sugar do most of the work. By coating your chopped fruit in sugar, the flavors are all pulled out over a period of about 30 minutes. Adding liqueurs or a spirit to a macerated syrup not only acts as a preservative; it also adds a boost of flavor. The combination of macerated starfruit and kumquat liqueur makes for a tropical, refreshing, and rich syrup. Starfruit are full of vitamin C, high in antioxidants, and have various other health benefits. Starfruit Syrup is used in the Startini (Chapter 8) to help cleanse and heal after a traumatic event.

YIELDS 4 OUNCES

1 large starfruit, sliced

1 cup granulated sugar

2 ounces kumquat liqueur

1. In a medium bowl, coat starfruit thoroughly first with sugar then with liqueur.
2. Allow to sit at least 30 minutes up to 3 hours.
3. Strain into a sealable container and store in refrigerator for up to 1 month.

CILANTRO SYRUP

Cilantro Syrup appears as a purifying agent for The Cleanse (Chapter 5). This is a cold syrup infusion, chosen to prevent the hot Simple Syrup from cooking the cilantro and changing the flavor. Cilantro rids the body of heavy metals; it is both an antioxidant and an antifungal. The list of beneficial properties goes on for this tiny, delicious, and magical herb. Speaking of magical, cilantro is good for making friends, for cleansing your aura, for protection, and even for fending off snakes.

1. In a sealable container, add Simple Syrup and cilantro. Close and shake briefly.

2. Store in a sealed container in refrigerator overnight. Strain mixture, then return to a sealed container and store in refrigerator for up to 2 weeks.

YIELDS 1 CUP

1 cup Simple Syrup (see recipe in Chapter 3)

2 tablespoons chopped fresh cilantro

CANDIED ORANGE WHEELS AND ORANGE SYRUP

This recipe makes two products: Candied Orange Wheels for garnish and Orange Syrup for mixing. Oranges represent and welcome abundance and are good luck signs for financial wealth to come. They are also used in love spells and spells requesting the strength of endurance during difficult times. All in all, oranges are versatile in spellwork.

———————

1. In a small saucepan, stir sugar and water over medium heat until sugar is dissolved. Reduce heat to low before adding orange wheels.

2. Allow to sit over low heat 1 hour and 15 minutes, flipping them over periodically, until oranges are translucent.

3. Remove from heat and place orange wheels on a parchment paper–lined wire rack. Let sit overnight, then store in a sealable container at room temperature for up to 4 days.

4. Store Orange Syrup in a sealed container in refrigerator for up to 1 week.

YIELDS 1 MEDIUM ORANGE WORTH OF CANDIED ORANGE WHEELS AND 2 CUPS ORANGE SYRUP

1 medium orange, ends trimmed, sliced into $\frac{1}{4}$"-thick slices

1 cup granulated sugar

1 cup filtered water

HIBISCUS GRENADINE

Hibiscus is used in three recipes in this section (Hibiscus Syrup and Hibiscus Salt) because this flower is more than a pretty jewel created by Mother Nature. Hibiscus petals have a delicious, tart flavor, and the flower cures menstrual cramps and lower abdominal pain and helps thin phlegm for those with chronic coughing conditions. Magically speaking, hibiscus is tied to attracting love and physical attraction. Using hibiscus in a love spell will help ensure that the connection made is full of passion and sexuality. Pomegranate juice richens and thickens the tartness of the hibiscus. Pomegranates are also steeped in a rich history of magic: They are the fruit of reincarnation, everlasting life, and fertility. You will find them featured prominently in the illustrations of the Rider–Waite tarot deck.

YIELDS 4 CUPS

2 cups pomegranate juice

2 cups granulated sugar

1 cup dried hibiscus flowers

1 ounce vodka

1 teaspoon orange blossom water

1. In a small saucepan, heat pomegranate juice over medium heat about 3 minutes or until warm. Add sugar and stir until dissolved.

2. Add remaining ingredients. Stir, then increase heat to high and bring to a boil.

3. Remove from heat and allow to cool about 2 hours. Strain with cheesecloth into a sealable container. Store refrigerated in container for up to 1 month.

MINT SYRUP

Mint Syrup is a must for any mojito drinker. This easy-to-make syrup amps up the mint flavors in any drink that traditionally calls for muddled mint like the Two of Pimm's Cups (Chapter 5). Replace your usual sugar with this syrup in your next mojito, and you won't ever go back. Magically, mint has been used to attract love and wealth, to protect, and to improve your overall well-being. In terms of health benefits, mint is more than a tasty way to improve your breath. It is a great source of vitamin A, which is good for eye health, and other nutrients. Many people use it to treat their digestive issues.

YIELDS 1 CUP

½ cup granulated sugar

½ cup filtered water

1 handful of mint, with stems

1. In a small saucepan, heat sugar and water over low heat and stir until sugar is dissolved. Add mint to cover top of liquid completely.

2. Bring mixture to a low boil, remove from heat, and cool about 1 hour.

3. Strain and store in a sealed container in refrigerator for up to 2 weeks.

PEAR SYRUP

Pears are more than tasty; they have strong symbolism in various cultures. Many cultures associate the pear with women, due to its female shape, and it is therefore also tied to fertility. Chinese mythology names pears and their trees as bringing forth immortality. In Greek and Roman mythology, pears are associated with Hera, Aphrodite, and Pomona. Pears were also once considered an exotic fruit of the wealthy elite, so they can be used for attracting generational wealth. Pears are rich in antioxidants and act as natural anti-inflammatories—just some of the health benefits of this truly magical and mystical fruit.

YIELDS 1 CUP

½ cup granulated sugar

½ cup filtered water

1 cup chopped pear (Bartlett recommended)

1. In a small saucepan, heat sugar and water over low heat, stirring until sugar is dissolved.

2. Add pear and increase heat to medium, bringing syrup to a low boil before turning to low heat again.

3. Allow to simmer 15 minutes.

4. Strain into a sealable container and discard pear pieces. Store in refrigerator for up to 1 week.

QUICK STRAWBERRY SHRUB

A bit different from syrups, shrubs are vinegar-based liquids made with sugar, fruit, vinegar, and water. They are a great way to wake up the palate and surprise drinkers. This Quick Strawberry Shrub tastes like a light vinaigrette. It is nonalcoholic, so it is a great option for mocktails. Magically speaking, strawberries bring forth fertility and dedication. They are survival plants and therefore impart that instinct when used in spellwork. This fruit is all about endurance and success through believing in yourself.

YIELDS 1 CUP

1 cup hulled and chopped fresh strawberries

½ cup granulated sugar

½ cup filtered water

⅜ cup white wine vinegar

1. In a medium saucepan, heat sugar, water, and strawberries over low heat, stirring until sugar is dissolved.

2. Continue to stir periodically for 15 minutes.

3. Strain with a fine-mesh strainer, pressing strawberries to express as much juice and sugar as you can.

4. Measure mixture and add half as much white wine vinegar (about ⅜ cup). Stir until well mixed.

5. Store in a sealed container in refrigerator for up to 2 weeks.

BUTTERFLY PEA FLOWER TINCTURE

Butterfly pea flowers have been used to create potent purple dyes for centuries. The flowers contain antioxidants and can lower blood pressure and improve skin and hair health. Magically speaking, butterfly pea flowers are used to create serenity, to enforce protection, and to attract love and transformation. This tincture can be used in small amounts to add a little purple magic to any drink.

YIELDS ½ CUP

4 ounces vodka

2 tablespoons butterfly pea flowers

1. Combine vodka and butterfly pea blossoms in a sealable container, shake, and allow to infuse 10 minutes.

2. Strain, pressing flowers to express as much of their dye as possible, into a sealable glass container.

3. Store at room temperature indefinitely.

SALT AND SUGAR RECIPES

Beyond syrups, you can use different salts and sugars to add some magic to the final touches of your cocktails. The following recipes are for garnishing and rimming cocktails and getting creative with homemade sugar cubes.

HIBISCUS SALT

Hibiscus is used for a multitude of magical purposes by any witch that can get their hands on it. While hibiscus is largely used in love spells, it is also helpful for maintaining health and wellness. For that reason, combining it with salt is a great way to enforce protection. Salt is a protective mineral, and many keep small piles of salt in the corners of their rooms to keep out spirits. Hibiscus Salt is tart and bright and protective against the darkness.

1. Use a mortar and pestle to crush salt and hibiscus petals into more of a powder consistency, but not too fine (a similar consistency to the salt).

2. Use your right hand to hold the pestle, telling the salt and hibiscus what you need them to do for you. Run the mixture through your fingers, repeating your needs.

3. Store in a sealed container in a dry place indefinitely.

YIELDS 1½ TABLESPOONS

1 tablespoon salt

1 teaspoon dried hibiscus petals

HOMEMADE PEYCHAUD'S BITTERS SUGAR CUBES

Peychaud's Bitters are the original American bitters. They were created in New Orleans by the apothecary Antoine Amédée Peychaud in the 1830s. This highly potent concoction gave birth to what is considered to be the first American cocktail, the Sazerac. The full recipe for Peychaud's Bitters is a secret, but the tasting notes are warm, herbal, and flattering alongside many spirits. Steeped in American history and all the fantastic witchcraft of New Orleans, Peychaud's brings magic wherever it is added.

1. Preheat oven to 170°F.

2. In a medium bowl, add sugar and bitters and mix thoroughly.

3. Use a small silicone spatula to firmly pack sugar into a silicone cube tray. Pre-measure your tray to know how big each cube is. You want to yield 2 ounces of flavored sugar total so a large tray will be too much. Smaller trays will just give you more cubes to add per drink.

4. Place tray on a baking sheet and bake 15 minutes.

5. Remove and allow to cool before using, about 4 hours up to overnight.

6. Store in a sealed container in a cool, dry place for up to 1 month.

YIELDS 2 OUNCES FLAVORED SUGAR

⅓ cup granulated sugar

10 dashes Peychaud's Bitters

DEHYDRATED CITRUS

Citrus has long been used in spellwork, with each type of citrus bringing its own elements. Lemon, for example, is used for attracting friendship but is also a heavy-hitting citrus for many witches as they cleanse, enhance, brighten, and even induce creativity. Limes are useful for protection and creating peace as well as being purifying agents. Oranges create abundance and are the citrus of wealth and means.

YIELDS AS MANY WHEELS AS YOU CUT

1 medium lemon, orange, or lime, sliced into 1/4"-thick slices

1. Preheat oven to lowest possible setting (170°F recommended).
2. Place sliced citrus on wax paper–lined baking sheet and place in oven.
3. Flip every 1–2 hours, making sure slices don't burn, until dehydrated, 4–6 hours.
4. Store in a sealable container at room temperature indefinitely.

THE NEXT STEPS OF MAGICAL MIXING

You know how to cleanse yourself, your deck, and your space. You know several spreads to choose from, and you have accumulated all the bar gear you need to start mixing at home. As you move on to Part 2, also keep in mind that when you open yourself up to perform a tarot reading, you are opening a portal and calling to your spirit guides to enter through it and join you for guidance. For this reason, you should not read tarot while drinking, as the alcohol clouds your mind, making you susceptible to negative entities attaching to you. You may reflect further on your interpretation of the card as you sip, but the practice of drawing and reading should be done beforehand. Now, let's begin crafting those divinely inspired cocktails! Turn the page to continue your delectable tarot journey.

PART 2

TAROT COCKTAILS

Your bartending essentials and understanding of tarot in hand, you are ready to explore—and imbibe—the cocktail tarot deck. The following chapters contain seventy-eight original recipes, each crafted in the image of a particular tarot card. Each recipe was thoughtfully inspired by the tarot, classic cocktails, and ancient magical herb practices. Each is a unique potion meant to help you accomplish the goals revealed by a specific tarot card, whether it's to heal you, encourage you, celebrate your achievements, or motivate you to move on from something that doesn't serve you.

This tasty journey begins with the Minor Arcana. There are more Minor Arcana cards in the tarot deck than Major Arcana, and they represent smaller life steps, so they are a good place to begin this journey. There are four suits in the Minor Arcana: Wands, Cups, Pentacles, and Swords. There are fourteen cocktails for each suit, for a total of fifty-six recipes. The Minor Arcana recipes are followed by recipes inspired by each of the twenty-two Major Arcana cards, which are rarer to pull than the Minor Arcana and represent monumental life changes and events. It's time to draw your card(s) and let your spirit guides be your bartending assistants.

CHAPTER 4

THE MINOR ARCANA: SUIT OF WANDS

LIQUID AMBITION

Sip this caffeinated cocktail while you plan your next big step, whether it be a personal hobby or new career path! The sweet Amarula soothes the bitterness of the coffee, making your challenging new venture a little easier, while the Becherovka adds a hint of orange, clove, and cinnamon to remind you that you, and your coffee, are anything but regular.

SERVES 1

2 ounces heavy cream

**½ ounce Simple Syrup
(see recipe in Chapter 3)**

**1 ounce Becherovka,
divided**

2 ounces Amarula

6 ounces hot, black coffee

1. Remove the spiral from a Hawthorne strainer and put it in a cocktail shaker. Add heavy cream, Simple Syrup, and $3/4$ ounce Becherovka. Shake vigorously without ice for several minutes until you can feel the liquid solidify into whipped cream.

2. In a toddy mug, add Amarula, remaining $1/4$ ounce Becherovka, and coffee. Stir lightly. Top with whipped cream mixture.

ACE OF WANDS

The Ace of Wands is about getting things started. It's not a guarantee of success; it's a guarantee that it's time to move forward. The road might be tough, but complacency is more dangerous than failure. The Ace of Wands reversed symbolizes that you are not thinking outside the box enough. Conventional methods of thinking and living are impeding your progress. You may also have lost emotional connections to people and activities and don't feel invested in much of anything right now.

Upright Meaning:
Creative or professional breakthrough, rising to a challenge, ambition.

Reversed Meaning:
Apathy, limited by conventional way of thinking, futility.

THE CHOICE

The Two of Wands is all about the freedom of making your personal choices: The Choice, therefore, is all about what you want. Would you like bourbon or vodka with your ginger beer? Bourbon offers rich, woody, and caramel flavors, while vodka blends perfectly with the spice of the ginger beer and warm herbal notes of the Angostura. The final choice of flavor, like the choice this card points to, is yours.

1. In a Collins glass, add bourbon or vodka, followed by Simple Syrup and lemon juice. Fill glass with ice, top with ginger beer, and float lemon wheel on top for garnish.

2. Add Angostura on top of lemon wheel. Stir before drinking, incorporating lemon wheel and bitters into the glass.

SERVES 1

2 ounces bourbon or vodka

½ ounce Simple Syrup (see recipe in Chapter 3)

½ ounce lemon juice

6 ounces ginger beer

1 lemon wheel

2 dashes Angostura bitters

TWO OF WANDS

The Two of Wands is about choices, but it is also about not taking the decisions you make lightly. It demands that you have a clear mind and stable mental state when deciding on which life path to take. If you don't decide with a clear mind, you may make the wrong choice. Weigh your options wisely: Your whole world is in your hands. If you pull this card reversed, you are fearing the change your life needs or you are making decisions without really stopping to think about all the possible consequences.

Upright Meaning:
Making a well-informed decision, understanding the weight of your choice, being clear-headed before choosing your next life path.

Reversed Meaning:
Fear of change, holding back, making choices without weighing all the options.

IF YOU DON'T DECIDE
WITH A CLEAR MIND, YOU MAY
MAKE THE WRONG CHOICE.

SOMETHING NEW THIS WAY COMES

Inspired by the adventurous spirit of the Three of Wands, this cocktail is refreshing and unique. It is a pink, low-alcohol libation meant to open your eyes to new experiences and potential by using less-common ingredients full of fresh, exciting flavors. Elderflower is a healing herb, incorporated in this cocktail to represent the healthy new direction you are headed in. Relax and enjoy this uncommon and delicious new tipple.

1. Add all ingredients except flower to a mixing glass with ice. Stir, and strain into a Nick and Nora glass.
2. Float flower on top for garnish.

SERVES 1

1½ ounces Cocchi Rosa

¾ ounce gin

½ ounce elderflower liqueur

1 edible pink flower (pansy or rose)

THREE OF WANDS

The Three of Wands appears to tell you that a new adventure is on the horizon. This reading could be about a trip or something larger, like making a scary personal or professional choice. Whatever the question is, the Three of Wands is telling you that the time is now to turn your back on your comfort zone and take the first step. Pulling this card reversed means that you are full of regret, probably from restricting yourself. This may be the result of a lack of self-esteem, or you may just be feeling particularly self-conscious and not confident right now.

Upright Meaning:
Traveling, growth, making personal and professional progress.

Reversed Meaning:
Regret, lack of self-confidence, restrictions.

STAND YOUR GROUND

It's important to stand up for yourself and protect what's yours, and this cocktail has the backbone to illuminate this lesson from the tarot. With roots in the classic Manhattan, this strong and stirred concoction is spicy and herbal with a hint of sweetness. Take notes from the way it stands alone—and stands strong.

1. Add all ingredients except cherry and orange swath to a mixing glass with ice. Stir.

2. Place cherry in a classic Manhattan glass. Strain cocktail over cherry.

3. Flame orange swath over cocktail and discard swath.

SERVES 1

1½ ounces rye

¾ ounce Cynar

1 barspoon cognac-based orange liqueur

1 Luxardo maraschino cherry

1 orange swath

SEVEN OF WANDS

The Seven of Wands appears to forewarn of a challenging time. This challenge will be an infringement on what is yours or what you've been working toward. This card tells you to stand your ground and protect what you've built. It won't be easy, but the good news is that you have what it takes to withstand the coming storm. The Seven of Wands tells you to have faith in your inner strength. If the Seven of Wands is reversed, it's a sign of defeat or resignation.

Upright Meaning:
Protecting what you've built, standing up for yourself, a challenge.

Reversed Meaning:
Resigning, giving up, being defeated.

TAKE THE SHOT

There is no more time to waste! Your energy is best spent in achieving a definitive goal, and Take the Shot will help motivate and energize you so that you can act quickly and precisely on this ambition. Use the energy from the espresso to give yourself the vivacity of the sweet, chocolaty chaser as you take the leap in confidence.

SERVES 1

½ ounce Amarula

½ ounce crème de cacao

1 ounce espresso

1. In a shot glass, add Amarula and crème de cacao. In a separate shot glass, add espresso.

2. Shoot espresso shot and chase with Amarula and crème de cacao shot.

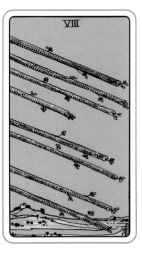

EIGHT OF WANDS

When you pull the Eight of Wands, the cards are telling you that it's time to act—and it's time to act quickly. Furthermore, this card is warning you of taking a shortcut, so don't assume fast action means cutting corners. The Eight of Wands still demands the work; it simply wants you to stop hesitating. If it appears to you reversed, you may have acted too slowly and missed a great opportunity. The reversed Eight of Wands could be telling you almost the opposite: You are acting too quickly and not thinking through options thoroughly enough.

Upright Meaning:
Quick action, a decisive and fast movement, confidence.

Reversed Meaning:
Impatience and overaction, hastiness, too slow to take a shot or opportunity.

THE CARDS ARE TELLING YOU THAT
IT'S TIME TO ACT—AND IT'S
TIME TO ACT QUICKLY.

THE WANDS OF REST

After putting it all on the line and working yourself to the bone in pursuit of a dream, you may stop moving long enough to realize how tired you are. The Wands of Rest is there for you to lean on in those moments following an endeavor. The chamomile will help you to achieve necessary rest, and the honey and lemon will soothe your stresses as you close your eyes and shut out the world for a bit of quiet relaxation.

1. Pierce lemon wheel with cloves, spacing them out where flesh meets pith.

2. In a toddy mug, add rye, Honey Syrup, lemon juice, and tea Float lemon wheel on top for garnish.

SERVES 1

1 lemon wheel

5 whole cloves

2 ounces rye

½ ounce Honey Syrup (see recipe in Chapter 3)

2 dashes lemon juice

6 ounces warm chamomile tea

NINE OF WANDS

The Nine of Wands represents a moment to breathe. The battle has been fought, the work has been done—now stop and relax. If you don't take care of yourself, you will work without improving, and the quality of your work will also suffer. So, listen to the Nine of Wands and take care of yourself. When reversed, this card signifies exhaustion, but unlike its upright position, it represents a refusal to take the necessary time to rest. This is going to result in *more* exhaustion, so if the card presents itself reversed, give yourself a respite: You won't regret it.

Upright Meaning:
Fatigue, exhausted, overworked.

Reversed Meaning:
Constant exhaustion, stubborn, will not take a break, stalemate.

FACE THE MUSIC

Daily struggles may be wearing you down, but the finish line is very close. Face the Music is a twist on the simple, classic Boilermaker. The two beverages in this recipe can either be sipped separately, or you can take the shot and then chase it with the beer. The combination is the perfect blend of simplicity and density: the spicy rye and roasty Guinness. Boilermakers are named for the people who used to have a shot and a beer at the end of their long shifts working engines all day. Let their practice of a simple drink combination propel you to the finish line. It may not be easy, but the result will be as delicious as the two components in this drink.

1. Pour Guinness into a pint glass. Pour rye into a shot glass.
2. Either shoot rye and chase it with Guinness, or sip each slowly.

SERVES 1

1 (16-ounce) can or bottle Guinness

1½ ounces rye

TEN OF WANDS

Pulling the Ten of Wands is a call to face what's weighing you down. While your journey is coming to an end, ignoring your burden won't be helpful in the long run. The Ten of Wands is challenging you to face your grief, whatever form it appears in. Your journey will be lighter once you do. Reversed, this card points out your refusal to take a break. If you don't listen to the card, you will burn out and your work and relationships will suffer.

Upright Meaning:
Exhaustion, a need to take a rest, an acceptance of taking a break.

Reversed Meaning:
Refusing to rest, burning out, losing grip because you refuse to take a break.

FACE WHAT'S WEIGHING YOU DOWN.
WHILE YOUR JOURNEY IS COMING TO
AN END, IGNORING YOUR BURDEN WON'T
BE HELPFUL IN THE LONG RUN.

THE SPICE OF LIFE

A daiquiri may be a classic cocktail, but this is not your average daiquiri. Inspired by the Page of Wands' promise of new beginnings, The Spice of Life has all the brightness of the traditional daiquiri with a spiciness that reminds you that life should be fun, exciting, and full of momentum forward.

---

1. Place Tajín on a small plate. Run lime wedge around the rim of a coupe glass. Dip rim in seasoning to coat. Discard lime.

2. Add remaining ingredients except jalapeño to a cocktail shaker filled with ice. Shake, and strain into rimmed glass.

3. Garnish with skewered pickled jalapeño.

SERVES 1

2 tablespoons Tajín seasoning

1 lime wedge, scored

2 ounces white rum

¾ ounce lime juice

½ ounce Simple Syrup (see recipe in Chapter 3)

¼ ounce Ancho Reyes liqueur

1 pickled jalapeño

PAGE OF WANDS

The Page of Wands is all about the excitement of something new: new beginnings, new journeys, new friends, new opportunities. If you've been feeling a need for change and pull the Page of Wands, this is your sign to move forward with that change. The Page of Wands is telling you that you are in fact ready, so embrace the change and be brave. If the Page of Wands is reversed, your fear of change is being pointed out by the cards. That fear is holding you back.

Upright Meaning:
Change, inspiration, free spirit, new beginning.

Reversed Meaning:
Fear of change, holding yourself back because of fear, boredom.

THE KNIGHT LIFE

This cocktail is a crushable blend of bright and bitter ingredients. While the Campari brings a hint of bitterness, it is balanced by the sweet brightness of the gin and lemon. Like the Knight of Wands, The Knight Life inspires your free spirit. Sip it in celebration of the adventurer within.

1. In a Collins glass, add gin, lemon juice, Campari, and Simple Syrup. Fill glass with ice and top with soda water.

2. Express orange swath over drink before putting it in cocktail. Stir before sipping.

SERVES 1

2 ounces gin

½ ounce lemon juice

½ ounce Campari

½ ounce Simple Syrup (see recipe in Chapter 3)

6 ounces soda water

1 orange swath

KNIGHT OF WANDS

The Knights in tarot are often symbols of travel and the need to leave the comfort of your nest. Therefore, the Knight of Wands is about time spent out of your comfort zone. It follows the energy and excitement for change of the Page of Wands. Pulling the Knight of Wands is a sign that this is a good time to spread your wings, travel, and take chances. If you pull the Knight of Wands reversed, you are feeling impatient or perhaps inadequate.

Upright Meaning:
Courage, free spirit, adventurer, traveler.

Reversed Meaning:
Lack of patience, afraid of change or to travel, feeling inadequate.

THE LIONESS

This variation of the classic Lion's Tail embodies the feminine fierceness of the Queen of Wands. It also pairs with its mate, A Lion's Tale (see recipe in this chapter), inspired by the King of Wands. Both cocktails include sunflower seeds, which ties them to the earth and fertility. They are also a nod to the Rider–Waite tarot deck, which features sunflowers on the Queen of Wands card. In spellwork, sunflowers are used for fertility, luck, fortune, and loyalty: all things the Queen of Wands encompasses.

---

1. Melt butter in a small pan over low heat. Add sunflower seeds and stir until toasted and brown, about 3 minutes. Remove from heat.

2. Add all ingredients except sunflower seeds to a cocktail shaker filled with ice. Shake, and strain into a coupe glass.

3. Garnish with toasted sunflower seeds.

SERVES 1

½ teaspoon salted butter

5 sunflower seeds

2 ounces bourbon

½ ounce Becherovka

½ ounce lime juice

½ ounce Simple Syrup (see recipe in Chapter 3)

¼ ounce Angostura bitters

QUEEN OF WANDS

When the Queen of Wands appears to you, it represents a strong feminine presence, someone to admire and look up to. This card is a symbol of strength and possibilities, and it represents being a stable, reliable person—someone who may even be intimidating because of their power. If reversed, the Queen of Wands represents someone who is passive. Pulling this card reversed is pointing out a flaw of someone who has refused to help themselves and others, and who is particularly unambitious when it comes to a career.

Upright Meaning:
Feminine strength, fertility, sexuality, ambition.

Reversed Meaning:
Passive, no ambition, weak, infertile, or impotent.

A LION'S TALE

A variation of the classic Lion's Tail, this cocktail embodies the boldness of the King of Wands suit. The sunflower seeds represent the tie of this King to the Queen of Wands: Both are symbols of potential, positivity, and leadership. Sunflowers are also used in magic work to increase loyalty, luck, and fertility—all things that both the Queen and King of Wands represent when pulled upright.

1. Melt butter in a small pan over low heat. Add sunflower seeds and stir until toasted and brown, about 3 minutes. Remove from heat.

2. Add all ingredients except sunflower seeds to a cocktail shaker. Dry shake. Add ice and shake 2 minutes.

3. Strain into a coupe glass. Garnish with toasted sunflower seeds

SERVES 1

½ teaspoon salted butter

5 sunflower seeds

2 ounces bourbon

¾ ounce Becherovka

½ ounce Simple Syrup
   (see recipe in Chapter 3)

½ ounce lime juice

1 large egg white

2 dashes Angostura bitters

KING OF WANDS

Your peers will recognize your leadership skills and creativity. It is time for you to take center stage and step into the role of the leader you've become. The King of Wands rules because of their confidence, skills, and positivity. This person is not a totalitarian, however; they lead by example and positive reinforcement. Reversed, the King of Wands is quite the opposite: controlling, self-centered, and arrogant. You could even call them a narcissist. This isn't someone to emulate or spend time around.

Upright Meaning:
Masculine and positive energy, creativity, leadership.

Reversed Meaning:
Controlling, arrogant, selfish, careless with others' feelings.

CHAPTER 5

MINOR ARCANA: SUIT OF CUPS

THE CLEANSE

It's time to put down old habits that aren't serving you; new, healthy ones are on the horizon. This mocktail cleanses toxins and former habits with cilantro, which detoxifies the body. The coconut water will refresh and hydrate you as you leave the old behind and prepare for the future promised in the Ace of Cups.

1. Add all ingredients except cilantro to a wine goblet. Stir lightly.
2. Express cilantro sprigs by slapping them lightly in your hands several times. Place them upright in drink.

SERVES 1

6 ounces coconut water

1 ounce Cilantro Syrup
   (see recipe in Chapter 3)

1 king cube

5 sprigs fresh cilantro,
   trimmed to the height of
   a wine goblet

ACE OF CUPS

It's a good time to release old routines and start new patterns. This could take the form of a burst of creativity, a new love on the horizon, or a sudden change of heart. Overall, it's a time to cleanse, heal, and prepare for something new concerning the heart. You don't have to know what that new thing is now, but you do need to prepare yourself for a release. If you pull the Ace of Cups reversed, you may be holding back emotionally, either consciously or subconsciously. The reversed Ace of Cups could also signify a refusal to change your former routines.

Upright Meaning:
Awakening, new beginnings due to letting go of old habits, the beginning of a love story, a sudden change of heart.

Reversed Meaning:
A refusal (but need) to let go, emotional loss, emotionally stunted.

TWO OF PIMM'S CUPS

The Two of Cups is all about the unity of two souls. So, enjoy this twist on a Pimm's Cup, full of mint and cucumber to refresh and fuel your new union with a loved one. Mint is a magical herb that attracts love and luck, while cucumbers represent inner and outer beauty, which is further positive energy to consume during this exciting time for you. These two magical elements blend to make a refreshing, lucky, and harmonious cocktail for two.

1. In a cocktail shaker, add Pimm's, Cucumber Syrup, Mint Syrup, and lemon juice. Fill with ice. Shake.

2. Strain into two Collins glasses. Fill with ice and top each glass with 4 ounces ginger ale.

3. Garnish with mint sprigs in drink and cucumber wheels on edge of glasses.

SERVES 2

4 ounces Pimm's No. 1

2 ounces Cucumber Syrup (see recipe in Chapter 3)

1 ounce Mint Syrup (see recipe in Chapter 3)

1 ounce lemon juice

8 ounces ginger ale

2 sprigs fresh mint

2 cucumber wheels, scored

TWO OF CUPS

The union represented by the Two of Cups could be romantic, platonic, or professional depending on the reading and where the card falls in your spread. Whatever the nature of the relationship, this is a positive card to pull. The relationship has balance, harmony, and mutual respect. This is also a new relationship, one that is going to blossom, and blossom beautifully. If reversed, the Two of Cups is all about dishonesty and broken trust. This could be because of adultery, greed, or deceit.

Upright Meaning:
Unity of two souls, balanced relationship, harmony.

Reversed Meaning:
Imbalance, distrust, broken relationship, greed.

BOTTOMS UP

It seems only right that the cocktail inspired by the pleasure-filled, celebratory Three of Cups includes champagne, the most decadent of the sparkling wines, and pear, a fruit that represents abundance, the female form (and therefore the holy feminine), and fertility. Use this bubbly indulgence to toast your abundance, in whatever form it might take.

1. Add pear liqueur and syrup to a champagne flute and top with champagne.

2. Garnish with pear slice in glass.

SERVES 1

½ ounce St. George Spiced Pear Liqueur

½ ounce Pear Syrup (see recipe in Chapter 3)

4 ounces champagne

1 pear slice

THREE OF CUPS

The Three of Cups is a celebration of a positive event that is related to relationships, as Cups are about love and human connections. It may be a wedding or a pregnancy, but whatever it is, it is likely a strongly feminine event, and it will give way to more celebrations. The Three of Cups reversed indicates an overindulgence that can lead to addiction issues, possibly alcoholism, as Cups are linked to water and liquid. Because it is a Cup card, it will affect relationships as well.

Upright Meaning:
Celebration, fertility, abundance, feminine energy.

Reversed Meaning:
Addiction to substances, overindulgence, wastefulness.

WHAT WAS MISSED

What Was Missed is a simple, eye-catching reminder to seize opportunities and not let them pass. The drink is blue, representing the element of water, which is associated with the Cups suit in tarot. It also has Suze to add a hint of bitterness and therefore also a warning against being overly bitter. Don't be like the Four of Cups: stubborn, resentful, and alone, missing out on what is passing you by.

1. Add all ingredients except lemon wheel to a mixing glass with ice. Stir, and strain into a classic Manhattan glass.

2. Skewer lemon wheel through pith and place in drink for garnish.

SERVES 1

1½ ounces blue curaçao

1 ounce vodka

½ ounce Suze

½ ounce Simple Syrup
(see recipe in Chapter 3)

1 lemon wheel

FOUR OF CUPS

When you pull the Four of Cups, it is important to consider why you have withdrawn from the world. This could be a valuable moment to re-establish priorities and do inner healing, but it could also be about hiding away and whether you've withdrawn for the wrong reasons. Withdrawing has also led to missed opportunities, which can lead to further withdrawing. If you pull the Four of Cups reversed, you are seizing the moment and taking advantage of an opportunity. It doesn't necessarily mean it will work out, but it is always a good thing to get out there and take a chance.

Upright Meaning:
Boredom, passing up opportunities, a time to recognize why you've withdrawn.

Reversed Meaning:
Action, seizing opportunity, getting out of a rut.

STILL STANDING

While everyone experiences losses that deserve time to grieve, there is still love, light, and possibility in the future. The Still Standing is a well-balanced reminder that even just a few quality ingredients can make something beautiful and delicious. Rejoice in this twist on the Manhattan cocktail and meditate on the blessings you have in your life.

* * *

1. Place cherry in a martini glass.
2. Add remaining ingredients to a mixing glass with ice. Stir, and strain over cherry.

SERVES 1

1 Luxardo maraschino cherry

2½ ounces bourbon

¾ ounce Bénédictine

2 dashes barrel-aged bitters

FIVE OF CUPS

The Five of Cups appears to tell you that your losses have been tremendous and valid, yes, but you must take the time to mourn and then move on. While three of the cups have spilled, two remain upright. Those cups need tending to, or they risk being tipped as well. If the Five of Cups is pulled reversed, you have done the work of mourning and are recovering from your trauma. You see the light at the end of the tunnel and have begun to move on and move forward.

Upright Meaning:
Loss, but still plenty to be thankful for; a reminder to focus on the positive; a time to mourn; guilt; shame.

* * *

Reversed Meaning:
Hope, recovering from loss, acceptance and moving on.

YOUR LOSSES HAVE BEEN
TREMENDOUS AND VALID, YES, BUT
YOU MUST TAKE THE TIME TO
MOURN AND THEN MOVE ON.

TRADITIONAL CUPS

Sip on Traditional Cups and be transported to positive childhood moments. A variation on the classic eggnog, the creamy, spiced flavors of this cocktail are meant to invite nostalgia, especially memories from beloved childhood holidays. Regardless of what treasured images this drink stirs up, honor the nostalgic Six of Cups with a delicious toast.

1. Add everything except cinnamon stick and 1 dash ground cinnamon to a cocktail shaker. Dry shake 1 minute. Add ice and shake 2 minutes.

2. Strain into a red wine glass or goblet. Garnish with remaining 1 dash cinnamon and cinnamon stick.

SERVES 1

2 ounces aged rum

1 ounce sweetened condensed milk

1 ounce Simple Syrup (see recipe in Chapter 3)

½ ounce brandy

½ ounce heavy cream

1 large egg

1 dash ground nutmeg

1 cinnamon stick

2 dashes ground cinnamon, divided

SIX OF CUPS

The Six of Cups represents a strong connection to your childhood and your inner child. This connection is valuable as you grow, but if you dwell *too* much on the past, you can forget to live in the present. The Six of Cups reversed may mean that you are not in touch with the innocence and wonder of your inner child, even though you may wish to be back in that time of your life. This reversed card could also be a good sign that you are leaving the comfort zone of your childhood and are moving on to new adventures.

Upright Meaning:
Nostalgia, childhood memories, in touch with your inner child, childish innocence.

Reversed Meaning:
Not being in touch with your inner child, dwelling on the past, moving away from your childhood comfort zone.

DREAMING WHILE AWAKE

Dreaming While Awake is as lofty as the card it is inspired by. It is blue for the water sign that Cups represent and fluffy like the clouds where your mind goes when you dream. The drink is made to foam up above the rim of the Collins glass, illustrating the heights your dreams can reach when unrestrained. It is inspired by a Ramos Gin Fizz, with its iconic fluffy heights.

1. Fill Collins glass with ice and water and place in freezer while following the next steps.

2. Add all ingredients except soda water and cherry to a cocktail shaker. Dry shake 30 seconds. Add ice to shaker and shake vigorously 2 minutes.

3. Remove Collins glass from freezer and empty.

4. Use a tea strainer and Hawthorne strainer to double-strain shaker into Collins glass. Slowly top with soda water. Drop cherry into glass.

SERVES 1

1½ ounces brandy

¾ ounce Simple Syrup (see recipe in Chapter 3)

½ ounce lemon juice

½ ounce blue curaçao

1 large egg white

3 ounces chilled soda water

1 Luxardo maraschino cherry

SEVEN OF CUPS

While the Seven of Cups holds promise and exciting aspirations, it can also represent confusion and poor decision-making. Pulling the Seven of Cups is the tarot telling you to make realistic goals and then put in the work to achieve them. Everything starts with a dream, but nothing happens without action. If you pull the Seven of Cups reversed, you have chosen an achievable goal and are making good plans for how to get there. However, this could also mean that you lack focus and are easily distracted because of it.

Upright Meaning:
Lofty goals—both achievable and unachievable, having goals you don't work toward.

Reversed Meaning:
Choosing a realistic goal and deciding to pursue it, distraction, confusion.

THE GREAT ESCAPE

Now is the time to walk away from a situation that you're already done with. For that purpose, this is a strong, stiff drink to put hair on your knuckles and give you the courage to move on. Its classic inspiration is the Toronto, which is a variation on the Manhattan. Having roots in two cocktails named for unique cities is yet another nod to the Eight of Cups, which incites you to exit your current circumstances and move on to something new.

SERVES 1

1 ounce rye

1 ounce Fernet-Branca

1 ounce sweet vermouth

1 orange swath

1. Add rye, Fernet-Branca, and vermouth to a mixing glass with ice. Stir, and strain into a rocks glass.
2. Flame orange swath over cocktail and discard.

EIGHT OF CUPS

The Eight of Cups appears when you need encouragement to leave a situation that no longer serves you. Turning your back on what you know might be scary or feel wrong, but it is the right thing to do. The Eight of Cups reversed means you are staying in a toxic situation, and you probably have been there for far too long already. What's holding you back from moving forward? Is it a refusal to accept that you're in a bad situation or a fear of failing when you leave? Whatever it is, it isn't worth staying put.

Upright Meaning:
Leaving a situation that no longer serves you, escaping, moving on.

Reversed Meaning:
Stagnation, staying in a situation that is not good for you anymore, pretending to be content when you aren't.

THE CUPS' ABUNDANCE

Have you been working intently toward a goal? Consider The Cups' Abundance your reward for your efforts. It mixes aged rye, representing your patience in creating something worthwhile, with the light and fruity tropical flavors of decadence. And while you drink this cocktail, it refills itself, demonstrating the bounty you have accumulated. You have earned this drink: enjoy it!

———————◆———————

1. Fill a rocks glass with crushed ice.

2. Add all ingredients to a cocktail shaker filled with ice and shake.

3. Using a small funnel, refill empty nip bottle with cocktail.

4. Pour remaining cocktail over crushed ice in glass.

5. Place your finger over the opening of the nip bottle and turn it over, gently placing it upside down in the crushed ice.

SERVES 1

1 (50ml) nip bottle rye

1½ ounces cherry liqueur

¾ ounce orgeat

¾ ounce Velvet Falernum

¾ ounce lemon juice

NINE OF CUPS

Unlike other cards that encourage new journeys without guaranteeing success, the Nine of Cups is a promise that your venture will be beneficial. You will plan, work, balance, and achieve. This doesn't mean the road will be easy, but it does mean it will be worth every step. Now you will get to enjoy all the benefits of your hard work. If you pull the Nine of Cups reversed, you have not achieved your goals and are left wanting more. Rather than dwelling on this, start making a new plan on how to turn things around.

Upright Meaning:
Your actions have a positive impact, positive results of your hard work, fortune.

———————◆———————

Reversed Meaning:
Dissatisfaction with current accomplishments, wanting more, a feeling of lacking something in your life.

CHAMPAGNE RAINBOW

Follow the lead of the Ten of Cups by raising a Rainbow Champagne to toast a bountiful future and comfortable present. Champagne Rainbow is a colorful cocktail inspired by the timeless Aperol Spritz. It maintains the bubbly, light flavors of the classic with additional notes from the grapefruit, which represents a time to shine and show self-love. Add some cocktail glitter to enjoy even more of the shimmery success you have earned.

1. Place grapefruit wheel in a red wine glass with a couple of ice cubes to keep it pressed against the glass.

2. Add remaining ingredients except cava and glitter to a cocktail shaker filled with ice. Shake, and pour with dirty rocks into wine glass. Add ice to fill.

3. Top with cava and cocktail glitter, if using.

SERVES 1

1 grapefruit wheel, sliced about ¼" thick

2 ounces ruby red grapefruit juice

1½ ounces vodka

1 ounce Aperol

1 ounce Simple Syrup (see recipe in Chapter 3)

¼ ounce lemon juice

4 ounces cava

1 barspoon red cocktail glitter (optional)

TEN OF CUPS

The Ten of Cups is a great omen. While you worked to get where you are, you can now breathe a little easier and celebrate your successes. This card is all about sharing and rejoicing in your personal and professional successes, particularly with family. If you pull the Ten of Cups reversed, you may be fighting with your family, likely over money. The sense of security from this card upright is pulled out from under you when it's reversed. There is no security, and so there is arguing. This could also result in a physical and emotional distance between you and your family.

Upright Meaning:
Celebration, financial security, strong family bonds.

Reversed Meaning:
Conflict, fighting with family, distance from loved ones due to arguing.

HERMES' MESSAGE

The Page of Cups brings a message of love and creativity, and is therefore named for the most famous messenger of all time: Hermes. As a nod to Hermes' Greek roots, this is an ouzo-based tipple, full of rich anise notes. Anise has many magical properties, from protection to better health to attracting love and friendship. So enjoy Hermes' Message as you prepare for an exciting invitation to arrive.

1. Add all ingredients except soda water and mint to a cocktail shaker. Dry shake.
2. Fill a Collins glass with pebble ice and pour contents of shaker over ice.
3. Top with soda water and garnish with mint sprig.

SERVES 1

1½ ounces ouzo

½ ounce Honey Syrup (see recipe in Chapter 3)

¼ ounce Bénédictine

4 ounces soda water

1 fresh mint sprig

PAGE of CUPS.

PAGE OF CUPS

The Page of Cups is a messenger of exciting things to come. Whether it's a new love, which the Page of Cups is often the harbinger of, or a new creative exploit, this Page is announcing it to you. Pulling this card is also a reminder to not take yourself so seriously; get in touch with your inner child to reinterpret the world through less judgmental eyes. When reversed, the Page of Cups is immature and childish. Reversed, this card serves as a warning to not focus so much on being noticed just to be noticed, but rather on doing something beneficial and interesting.

Upright Meaning:
New beginnings, especially concerning love; good news and opportunities ahead; a burst of creativity.

Reversed Meaning:
Emotional immaturity and vulnerability, childish, attention-seeking, irresponsible.

THE KNIGHT'S SOUR

Embodying the romance and creativity of the Knight of Cups, this whiskey sour variation has the bright notes of a sour complemented by the orange notes of Amaro Nonino. Oranges are used in magic to bring forth joy and love and all the warmth of the sun. The Amaro Nonino rounds the flavor of the traditional whiskey sour, making this cocktail new, bright, and warm, just like the Knight of Cups.

1. Add all ingredients except bitters to a cocktail shaker and dry shake. Add ice and shake again.

2. Strain into a coupe glass. Using a straw, extract 5 drops of bitters 1 drop at a time and top the cocktail with the droplets, evenly spaced out. Then, using a toothpick or skewer to drag droplets outward, make swirling designs of your choice with the bitters.

SERVES 1

2 ounces Amaro Nonino

¾ ounce Simple Syrup (see recipe in Chapter 3)

½ ounce lemon juice

½ ounce lime juice

1 large egg white

5 drops Peychaud's Bitters

KNIGHT OF CUPS

The Knight of Cups is a messenger with an invitation, telling you to let go of your insecurities and move forward with your dreams. This card also represents a lover or person with a strong artistic, romantic, and feminine energy. The Knight of Cups appears to invite you to an adventure of romance and creativity. When reversed, the Knight of Cups is jealous and unpredictable. This card reversed points out your lack of focus and resulting inability to finish projects.

Upright Meaning:
Romance, an artist, a sensitive soul.

Reversed Meaning:
Jealous, lack of follow-through, emotional instability.

THE QUEEN'S MIRROR

With the watery blue hue of curaçao symbolizing your psychic ability and the subconscious, The Queen's Mirror reflects how the Queen of Cups encourages you to trust your intuition. Your guides are telling you that if you lean on the positive influences around you, you will achieve emotional stability and will have a bright future because of it. Enjoy this beautiful and tasty reminder to stay grounded and maintain balance.

1. Add all ingredients except cherry to a cocktail shaker filled with ice. Shake, and strain into a coupe glass.

2. Garnish with skewered cherry.

SERVES 1

1½ ounces London dry-style gin

¾ ounce lime juice

½ ounce blue curaçao

½ ounce orgeat

1 Luxardo maraschino cherry

QUEEN OF CUPS

Pulling the Queen of Cups is a positive sign. The Queen represents a maternal influence in your life. This person is intuitive, introspective, and empathetic. They have mastered emotional maturity but still must reach mastery of the Pentacles, Wands, and Swords before becoming The Empress of the Major Arcana. In reverse, this card is a reminder to balance your emotions with your rational thoughts.

Upright Meaning:
Intuition, empathy, emotional control.

Reversed Meaning:
Emotional avoidance, overwhelmed, imbalance of heart and brain.

THE KING'S REFLECTION

In spellwork, basil heals, helps in astral projection, and brings about relaxation. Its presence in this drink is meant to bring you all of those things, swirled into an exquisite cocktail. The King's Reflection inspires with its unusual blend of herbal, sweet, and vinegary flavors. Just like this cocktail, you are in for some unexpected flavors, should you draw the King of Cups.

---

1. In a Collins glass, add shrub, rum, and lemon juice. Add ice to fill.
2. Top with white wine. Express basil over drink and place in glass for garnish.

SERVES 1

2 ounces Quick Strawberry Shrub (see recipe in Chapter 3)

1½ ounces white rum

1 dash lemon juice

4 ounces dry sparkling white wine

1 sprig or large leaf fresh basil

KING OF CUPS

Pulling the King of Cups is a sign of someone with positive abilities. They can control their emotions and use their intuition to make informed decisions. This person is a great role model, and you could learn a lot from emulating them in their emotional intelligence. If pulled reversed, the King of Cups is emotionally unstable and therefore bad at making decisions. This person reacts too quickly and often incorrectly and can at times be withdrawn, likely because they know they tend to overreact.

Upright Meaning:
Mastery of emotions, control, intuition, good decision-making skills.

Reversed Meaning:
No control of emotions, reactive, withdrawn, poor decision-making skills.

CHAPTER 6

MINOR ARCANA: SUIT OF PENTACLES

ACE OF THE EARTH

A financial or material gift has been foretold in the cards. Ace of the Earth features beet juice, a true bounty of the soil. Beets represent health, sustenance, and future success. The mezcal and honey are also plant-based "fruits" of the planet. Enjoy this earthy, well-rounded cocktail as you plan for your future. It is just the treat you deserve to manifest an exciting piece of earthly reward.

1. Add king cube to a goblet or red wine glass.
2. Add remaining ingredients to a cocktail shaker filled with ice. Shake, and strain into goblet or glass.

SERVES 1

1 round king cube

2 ounces mezcal

1 ounce beet juice

3/4 ounce Honey Syrup
(see recipe in Chapter 3)

1/2 ounce lemon juice

ACE OF PENTACLES

The Ace of Pentacles means that an unexpected financial gain, gift, or opportunity is coming your way. This is the result of manifestation and a little bit of luck. Use the energy of this gift to move yourself forward. More excitement awaits you if you stay focused and positive. If reversed, you have missed a chance to get material gain. You may have even lost money or a large, valuable possession. However, you have the ability to overcome this challenge and regain financial stability. Keep your greed in check as well if you pull the Ace of Pentacles reversed.

Upright Meaning:
Manifestation, wealth, financial stability, material gain.

Reversed Meaning:
Missed opportunity, financial or material loss, greed, poverty.

THE TWO-HEADED SNAKE

Like the Two of Pentacles, The Two-Headed Snake is about balance. Two spirits take center stage in this cocktail. They work well together, but either could also stand on its own or do well mixed with other ingredients. While The Two-Headed Snake is delicious, the potential beyond it is also enticing.

SERVES 1

1 tablespoon green-colored granulated sugar

1 lime wedge, scored

1½ ounces white rum

1½ ounces Amaretto

1. Pour sugar on a small plate. Run lime wedge around half of the rim of a classic Manhattan glass. Dip rim in sugar to coat. Discard lime.

2. Add remaining ingredients to a mixing glass with ice. Stir, and strain into rimmed Manhattan glass.

TWO OF PENTACLES

The Two of Pentacles is all about the juggling act that many of us perform in our lives. While the card shows success in achieving balance, the act cannot sustain itself. You can't excel at two things at the same time; you must prioritize and focus on one goal at a time. If you pull this card reversed, you are not juggling well enough. You have no focus, and you are losing ground—likely financially—because of your inability to manage responsibilities.

Upright Meaning:
A juggling act of focus and responsibilities, choosing one focus, balancing many responsibilities well.

Reversed Meaning:
A lack of focus, unhappiness, mismanaged life, loss of finances.

3 BECOME 1

Inspired by the successful collaboration symbolized in the Three of Pentacles, 3 Become 1 is a harmony of three unique ingredients working together to make an exciting and unique cocktail. Like the Three of Pentacles, each ingredient in this harmonious libation brings forth its own flavors to create one successful, balanced collaboration.

Add all ingredients to a mixing glass with ice. Stir, and strain into a classic Manhattan glass.

SERVES 1

1 ounce aged rum

¾ ounce Cardamaro

½ ounce Bonal

1 dash black walnut bitters

THREE OF PENTACLES

The success of the Three of Pentacles is one of financial and/or material gain. If the Three of Pentacles appears to you, it's telling you that your new venture with others has excellent potential for financial rewards. Every member of the team has or will bring their specialties to the table, and everyone respects and takes opinions into consideration. This type of symbiotic relationship is rare and is bound to bring forth good things. However, if reversed, the card means quite the opposite. No team project will go well, for one reason or another, if you pull the Three of Pentacles reversed. This is a time to pursue your next project solo.

Upright Meaning:
A successful group project, working well together, creating financial gain from good teamwork.

Reversed Meaning:
Lack of teamwork, discontent in a team project, an independent venture rather than group project.

FOUR FENCES

The Four of Pentacles is a card of greed and withholding, and as such, this drink is all about those sentiments of grasping what is yours, without any charity or sense of selflessness. It contains two kinds of amari, which are Italian bitters, which represent the concept of bitterness and greed in this card. Warm flavors with hints of clove, a spice with magical properties in protection, celebrate the positive aspect of this card: setting boundaries. Take a hint from the Four of Pentacles and reflect on your own boundaries as you stir and strain its mystically inspired cocktail.

SERVES 1

1 ounce Amaro Averna

3/4 ounce reposado tequila

3/4 ounce Cardamaro

1 dash orange bitters

1 king cube

1 Candied Orange Wheel (see recipe in Chapter 3)

1. Add all ingredients except king cube and orange wheel to a mixing glass with ice. Stir, and strain over king cube in a rocks glass.

2. Garnish with orange wheel skewered through pith.

FOUR OF PENTACLES

The Four of Pentacles represents greed and financial boundaries, but it can also be about necessary boundaries of self-protection. Consider if you're being stingy or healthy. It might be time to cut someone off who is a financial burden, or to dig into your savings and give back to the community or to a friend in need. When in reverse, the Four of Pentacles is telling you to rein in your spending. This could be a warning of future financial loss if you don't change your spending habits. However, it could also be commending your generosity for a recent financial donation.

Upright Meaning:
Greed, financial withholding, setting boundaries.

Reversed Meaning:
Overspending, generosity, financial loss.

IT MIGHT BE TIME TO CUT SOMEONE OFF
WHO IS A FINANCIAL BURDEN,
OR TO DIG INTO YOUR SAVINGS AND
GIVE BACK TO THE COMMUNITY OR
TO A FRIEND IN NEED.

MULLED-OVER WINE

Made of common ingredients, nothing particularly fancy or expensive, this drink is easily shared and not to be worried about. It is simply meant to comfort your soul and insides with both literal warmth and the metaphorically warm flavors of cloves, star anise, and brandy. Sip a mug of Mulled-Over Wine and forget your troubles for a moment: The Five of Pentacles asks that you give more attention to your blessings than your anxieties for once.

SERVES 2

2 cups dry red wine

½ cup dark brown sugar

¼ cup orange juice

1 tablespoon whole cloves

12 whole star anise pods, divided

½ cup brandy

1. In a small saucepan, combine wine, sugar, orange juice, cloves, and 10 of the star anise pods over low heat until sugar is dissolved.

2. Keep on low heat and stir periodically for 15 minutes. Remove from heat and add brandy.

3. Stir, and strain spices out. Serve hot in two toddy mugs with remaining 2 star anise pods floating on top for garnish.

FIVE OF PENTACLES

The Five of Pentacles is a card of either not having financial means or concerning yourself with the fear of not having financial means to the point that you forget what you already have. Whether it is upright or reversed, it calls attention to the human tendency to focus on either wants or worries above the blessings already obtained. If you pull this card, refocus your energy on your loved ones and the other positives in your life. Know that financial difficulties will pass, and you will persevere.

Upright Meaning:
Financial ruin or fear of experiencing financial ruin, forgetting your current blessings due to worry, anxiety.

Reversed Meaning:
Persevering through a difficult financial time, financial recovery, focusing too much on wants and forgetting your blessings.

SILVER CHARITY

The Six of Pentacles is a card of giving and charity, and so this cocktail is crafted to share and sparkle. The sherry and Lillet Blanc make Silver Charity light and wine-based, with the floral notes of the elderflower liqueur offering hints of a fruitful spring to come. The cava adds celebratory shine, along with the cocktail glitter.

1. Add all ingredients except cava to a mixing glass with ice. Stir, then strain into two champagne flutes.

2. Top each flute with 2 ounces cava.

SERVES 2

3 ounces manzanilla sherry

1 ounce elderflower liqueur

1 ounce Lillet Blanc

2 barspoons silver cocktail glitter

4 ounces cava

SIX OF PENTACLES

The Six of Pentacles is a relief that follows the struggle of the Five of Pentacles. It indicates a time when you will either be given charity or be able to give charity. If you pull this card and times have been tough, you can expect someone to help you out now. If you pull this card and have been financially stable, it's time to look around and see what you can do for others. Reversed, this card is more about withholding money. You should stop and see if you could do something for others, but also consider if you need help from someone who isn't offering it despite being financially able to do so.

Upright Meaning:
Charity, selflessness, either giving or receiving generosity.

Reversed Meaning:
Selfishness, greed or withholding money, imbalance of power.

YOU WILL EITHER BE GIVEN CHARITY OR
BE ABLE TO GIVE CHARITY.

THE SEEDS OF PENTACLES

It's important to maintain the seeds you've planted. While now is a time to wait, you must not forget to put in the daily work on your projects for them to blossom fully. This cocktail is reminiscent of a garden with flavors of caraway, carrots, and rye. It elicits the flavors of a fruitful harvest for you to enjoy while you watch your actual project grow.

———— ◆ ————

Add all ingredients to a cocktail shaker filled with ice. Shake, and strain into a coupe glass.

SERVES 1

1½ ounces applejack whiskey

1 ounce carrot juice

½ ounce Kümmel

½ ounce Honey Syrup (see recipe in Chapter 3)

SEVEN OF PENTACLES

The Seven of Pentacles is a positive card to pull upright. It's making sure you know that your long-term planning skills are on point; all you need to do is maintain your follow-through. If this card is reversed, you may have experienced success, but it will be short-lived due to poor long-term planning. The Seven of Pentacles tells you to learn from your mistakes for the future. Upright or reversed, this card urges you not to give up.

Upright Meaning:
A time to be patient, continue watering your metaphorical seeds for them to grow, keep paying attention to your passion project, working toward your long-term goals.

———— ◆ ————

Reversed Meaning:
Poor planning toward long-term goals, only short-term success, poor financial planning, lack of follow-through.

THE HARVEST

The base of this cocktail is like the fruits of a harvest, which take time to bloom. It is an aged rye, matured in a barrel for four years before being released into the world. Just as a current project is taking time and patience, so has this rye. The Kümmel is a rewarding blend of sesame, poppy, onion, and pepper flavors. Enjoy The Harvest, a cocktail meant to showcase the results promised by the Eight of Pentacles, while you work on your own personal harvest.

1. Add all ingredients except cherry to a mixing glass with ice. Stir, and strain into a classic Manhattan glass.

2. Garnish with skewered cherry.

SERVES 1

1½ ounces Templeton 4 Year Rye

¾ ounce sweet vermouth

½ ounce Kümmel

2 dashes sarsaparilla bitters

1 Luxardo maraschino cherry

EIGHT OF PENTACLES

When you pull the Eight of Pentacles upright, you are in for an excellent payoff. This won't be charity, and it won't be a surprise; it will be the well-earned rewards of your hard work, planning, and patience. This has been an excellent learning experience for you regarding the value of these three attributes. Carry these lessons with you into your next steps of life. In reverse, the Eight of Pentacles signifies a lack of follow-through and missed opportunities. You haven't planned well or put in the work necessary to reap the benefits of your idea. Take this as a sign to learn from your mistakes.

Upright Meaning:
Harvest, ambition, hard work toward a goal, skillful commitment, excellent follow-through.

Reversed Meaning:
Lazy or without ambition, lack of follow-through when opportunities knock, no forethought, cutting corners.

YOU ARE IN FOR AN EXCELLENT PAYOFF. THIS WON'T BE CHARITY, AND IT WON'T BE A SURPRISE; IT WILL BE THE WELL-EARNED REWARDS OF YOUR HARD WORK, PLANNING, AND PATIENCE.

FRUIT OF THE VINE

A sippable embodiment of the Nine of Pentacles' wealth and relaxation, Fruit of the Vine is all about enjoying the finer things in life. It features citrus and overproof rum, topped with a dry red wine, and is a twist on a New York Sour. This cocktail is like the tarot card: meant to be enjoyed slowly. You have earned it. Consider a purple, white, or yellow edible flower. Purple represents royalty, white represents a clean slate and removal of old energy, and yellow represents new growth and energy.

1. Add all ingredients except wine and flower to a cocktail shaker filled with ice. Shake, and pour with dirty rocks into a wine goblet. Add fresh ice to fill.

2. Carefully pour wine on top of the drink so it floats. Garnish with edible flower.

SERVES 1

1 ounce overproof rum

1 ounce white rum

1½ ounces Simple Syrup (see recipe in Chapter 3)

½ ounce Honey Syrup (see recipe in Chapter 3)

½ ounce lemon juice

½ ounce lime juice

2 ounces dry red wine (Cabernet Sauvignon recommended)

1 edible flower in color of choice

NINE OF PENTACLES

The Nine of Pentacles is a completion card that signifies a time to rest and relax. This time was well earned with hard work and dedication. The fruits of your labors are all around you, creating a comfortable and stable environment. The Nine of Pentacles appearing in a reading is telling you to enjoy yourself now. If the Nine of Pentacles is reversed, you're guilty of poor financial planning and likely overspending as well. You haven't put in the work, but you still want to play.

Upright Meaning:
Enjoying the rewards of hard work, wealth, financial stability, good investment(s).

Reversed Meaning:
Overspending, poor financial planning, financial instability and loss, bad investment(s).

PENTACLE INHERITANCE

Crafted in the image of the Ten of Pentacles' transcendent financial success, the Pentacle Inheritance is a rich cocktail made with añejo tequila and hibiscus. The purply hue of the Hibiscus Grenadine is a nod to the affluence of royalty, and the aged tequila offers a rich base for this elevated twist on a classic margarita.

SERVES 1

**2 tablespoons Hibiscus Salt
(see recipe in Chapter 3)**

1 lime wedge, scored

1½ ounces añejo tequila

**1 ounce Hibiscus Grenadine
(see recipe in Chapter 3)**

¾ ounce lime juice

1. Pour salt onto a small plate. Run lime wedge around the rim of a rocks glass. Dip rim in salt to coat. Discard lime.

2. Add remaining ingredients to a cocktail shaker filled with ice and shake. Pour with dirty rocks into rimmed rocks glass.

TEN OF PENTACLES

The Ten of Pentacles shows that the hard work you've put in will lead you to a level of success that transcends generations. This may mean the small business you've started will one day go to your children or siblings' children. Or perhaps you will be able to create trust funds for the youths in your family. This card may also indicate a family inheritance for you. Reversed, the Ten of Pentacles indicates turmoil, arguments, and financial difficulties. This is the type of hardship that will impact the whole family and will likely involve an inheritance.

Upright Meaning:
Generational wealth, financial stability, family wealth, affluence, inheritance.

Reversed Meaning:
Debt, family turmoil and confrontations over money, financial success but only for the short term.

BEGIN AGAIN

Manifesting the fresh start of the Page of Pentacles, Begin Again is a play on the classic Kir Royale. Traditionally a brunch cocktail, this variation is the beginning of a new adventure, just as brunch is the (delicious) beginning of a new day. It includes a luscious raspberry liqueur, representing maturing and moving forward, with champagne as a nod to the celebratory nature of beginning a new and exciting chapter.

SERVES 1

¼ ounce raspberry liqueur

5 ounces champagne

1 fresh raspberry

Add raspberry liqueur to a champagne flute, then top with champagne. Garnish with skewered raspberry.

PAGE OF PENTACLES

The Page of Pentacles indicates a new opportunity that you should take. The Pages are young messengers, bringing invitations to the next adventure. This Page is telling you that an opportunity involving money and/or material gain is on the horizon for you, and that you should take it. This card does not guarantee success; that's something you will achieve if you put in the work. When in reverse, the Page of Pentacles is a warning of irresponsible behavior and lack of direction. Do some inner reflecting to see where you could use more direction in your life.

Upright Meaning:
A new beginning or learning opportunity, new goals, putting together plans for the future.

Reversed Meaning:
Aimlessness, no prospects, not taking responsibility.

THE KNIGHT'S HIBISCUS GIMLET

Worthy of the dutiful Knight of Pentacles, this cocktail is a tart interpretation of a vodka gimlet, a simple and straightforward classic. The Knight's Hibiscus Gimlet has an added richness from the dry curaçao and Hibiscus Grenadine, signifying the rewards of finishing your task at hand. Hibiscus brings love and lust, so don't lose heart over the Knight of Pentacles: Happy times lie ahead if you focus on finishing the job at hand.

1. Add all ingredients except flower to a cocktail shaker filled with ice. Shake, and strain into a coupe glass.
2. Float flower on top for garnish.

SERVES 1

1½ ounces vodka

¾ ounce lime juice

½ ounce Simple Syrup (see recipe in Chapter 3)

½ ounce dry curaçao

½ ounce Hibiscus Grenadine (see recipe in Chapter 3)

1 edible pink flower (pansy or rose)

KNIGHT OF PENTACLES

The Knight of Pentacles is about a necessary routine. You may be feeling dissatisfied or in a rut, but certain duties just need to be taken care of. The Knight of Pentacles represents that feeling of routine in order to achieve goals and also the desire for something more. This Knight is telling you to keep doing what you're doing: You're on the right path; it's just a little hard to see the light at the end of the tunnel right now. When reversed, the Knight of Pentacles is lazy and stubborn. There is an irresponsibility to this card when drawn reversed.

Upright Meaning:
Dissatisfied, responsibility, hard work, finishing what you started.

Reversed Meaning:
Stubborn, lazy, irresponsible.

YOU'RE ON THE RIGHT PATH;
IT'S JUST A LITTLE HARD TO SEE
THE LIGHT AT THE END OF THE TUNNEL
RIGHT NOW.

THE SHIMMERING BREADWINNER

Inspired by banana bread, the vanilla and walnut flavors of this cocktail are warm and soft, like the maternal, feminine Queen of Pentacles. The cocktail glitter that adorns The Shimmering Breadwinner represents the wealth of this tarot card. This Queen and their cocktail are inviting and comforting.

1. Add rum, banana liqueur, Velvet Falernum, vanilla, and about $3/4$ of the cocktail glitter to a mixing glass with ice.

2. Stir, and strain over king cube in a coupe glass. Sprinkle remaining cocktail glitter on cube for garnish.

SERVES 1

1½ ounces white rum

¾ ounce banana liqueur

½ ounce Velvet Falernum

1 dash vanilla extract

1 heaping barspoon gold cocktail glitter, divided

1 king cube

QUEEN OF PENTACLES

The Queen of Pentacles, like all Queens in the Minor Arcana, is a strong feminine force. This person is maternal, financially stable, and willing and able to care for others. They are the breadwinner, the boss—even when reversed. This Queen reversed is simply in a moment where they need to take care of themselves and exercise independence. A reversed card could mean rocky financial times as well, so check your investments.

Upright Meaning:
Financial stability, feminine strength, maternal, affection, warmth.

Reversed Meaning:
Independence, self-care, imbalance between work and home life, financial instability.

THE KING'S PYRITE

This cocktail glistens like the gold in the wealthy and masculine King of Pentacles' bank account. Lavender attracts money, and the gold cocktail glitter, inspired by the pyrite crystal, represents riches. An elevated invitation of wealth, it's only the best of the best for this affluent ruler and those who draw this card in a reading.

1. Add all ingredients except wine, lavender buds, and cocktail glitter to a cocktail shaker filled with ice. Shake, and strain into a martini glass.

2. Top with wine and sprinkle lavender buds and glitter on top for garnish.

SERVES 1

1½ ounces moonshine

¾ ounce Lavender Honey Syrup (see recipe in Chapter 3)

¼ ounce lemon juice

2 ounces dry white wine (pinot grigio recommended)

1 barspoon dried lavender buds

1 barspoon gold cocktail glitter

KING OF PENTACLES

The King of Pentacles is a wealthy person with a strong masculine energy. They are wise and intelligent with plenty of money to take care of others, which they do gladly. This King has a keen sense for business, so if they represent a person in your life and their business interests you, ask them to take you under their wing. If this financially versed person is you, keep on the same path. You are a caretaker and a leader. If you pull this King reversed, it signifies that you are overtaken by selfishness and greed. You are a good businessperson, but at what cost?

Upright Meaning:
Affluence, wisdom, financial stability, a desire to care for others with one's wealth, a good sense of business.

Reversed Meaning:
Greedy, relentless businessperson, poor investment choices, selfish.

CHAPTER 7

MINOR ARCANA: SUIT OF SWORDS

A MOMENT OF CLARITY

A Moment of Clarity reflects a sense of seeing things exactly as they are—as the Ace of Swords knows you can see them. For that reason, this drink is completely transparent, like water, so that you can see through to the heart of the matter, which is represented by the maraschino cherry. So, sip this clear blend of citrus and floral elements and trust what you see. You're looking right through to the situation at hand.

1. Skewer cherry and place on rim of a martini glass.

2. Add remaining ingredients to a mixing glass with ice. Stir, and strain into glass.

SERVES 1

1 Luxardo maraschino cherry

2 ounces gin

¾ ounce Lillet Blanc

½ ounce elderflower liqueur

½ ounce vodka

3 dashes grapefruit bitters

ACE OF SWORDS

The Ace of Swords represents a vision in your higher consciousness. Pulling this card is a sign to trust what your instincts are pointing you to. This is a moment of clear thought that you should trust. What is your gut telling you to see or do? Reflect, and make a new or revised plan. Reversed, the Ace of Swords is about foggy judgment and bad decision-making due to confusion and an inability to think clearly.

Upright Meaning:
Mental clarity, vision, a breakthrough after thorough reflection.

Reversed Meaning:
Poor judgment, inability to think clearly, confusion, hostility.

THE STALEMATE

Have you found yourself caught in the middle of something? A variation of a shandy, The Stalemate combines two concepts in one to reflect the impasse you face. Draw your sword or, rather, your mixing ingredients, and make your move: Combine the lager with the cocktail and embrace the gray area for a moment.

SERVES 1

1 ounce bourbon

½ ounce acai liqueur

½ ounce ginger liqueur

5 ounces lager

1. In a Collins glass, add bourbon and liqueurs. Fill glass with ice.
2. Top glass with lager and stir lightly.

TWO OF SWORDS

The Two of Swords represents a person being forced to either make a decision without all the information or to make a decision that they refuse to make. (This is represented by the blindfolded person depicted on the card.) If upright, you are lacking information either consciously or unconsciously to make the right call. If reversed, the blindfold can help you quiet the outside world around you and reflect on the right answer. No matter the circumstances, a decision must be made.

Upright Meaning:
Stagnation, stalemate, being caught in the middle, painful decisions ahead, questions of where your loyalty lies, needing to choose but refusing to, being metaphorically blindfolded.

Reversed Meaning:
Seeing the truth, being deceived, choosing a side, being metaphorically blindfolded.

THE HEARTBREAK

Red like a broken heart, this cocktail embodies the heartbreak of the Three of Swords. The bright lime and pineapple greet you with the tequila upfront, but in the end, the drink is surprisingly yet deliciously bitter from the Carpano Botanic finishing the last sips. This drink is the journey of an ill-fated love: sweet and fun, with an unexpected ending.

1. Pour Carpano Botanic into a rocks glass and add king cube on top.
2. Add remaining ingredients to a cocktail shaker filled with ice. Shake, and strain over king cube into rocks glass.

SERVES 1

1 ounce Carpano Botanic

1 king cube

2 ounces añejo tequila

¾ ounce pineapple juice

½ ounce Simple Syrup (see recipe in Chapter 3)

½ ounce lime juice

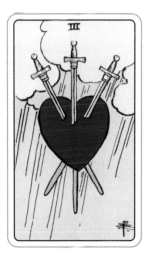

THREE OF SWORDS

The Three of Swords refers to a harsh reality of the human experience: trauma. When you pull the Three of Swords, it is a warning about lies and heartbreak: Either they will be inflicted on you or you will inflict them on others. Remember that like all hardships, this difficulty will pass with time. Reversed, the Three of Swords may mean that the negativity you're feeling is aimed inward, and you should try to forgive yourself and practice self-love. It could also mean that you are healing after a traumatic event, particularly a breakup or loss of a relationship.

Upright Meaning:
Lies, deceit, adultery, heartbreak, loss.

Reversed Meaning:
Reconciliation, a time of healing after trauma, self-hatred.

A MINDFUL REST

The cards have asked that you pause in your routine to regroup your mental and spiritual self. A Mindful Rest is here to help you achieve this restfulness with its take on a nonalcoholic hot toddy. The Seedlip brings grassy, green notes that are complemented by the rich, calming Chamomile Syrup. This treat won't cloud your mind but will encourage it to relax and regroup, having a mindful rest.

1. Place Seedlip Garden 108 Nonalcoholic Distilled Spirits, Chamomile Syrup, lemon juice, and hot water in a toddy mug. Stir briefly.

2. Express lemon swath over mug.

3. Cut lemon swath on edges to make line straight and angle ends. Pierce with cloves and drop into mug.

SERVES 1

1 ounce Seedlip Garden 108 Nonalcoholic Distilled Spirits

½ ounce Chamomile Syrup (see recipe in Chapter 3)

2 dashes lemon juice

8 ounces hot filtered water

1 lemon swath

3 whole cloves

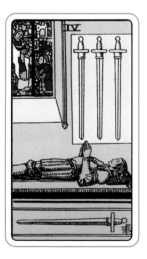

FOUR OF SWORDS

The Four of Swords indicates it's time for you to seclude yourself, meditate, sleep, and get back in touch with your inner self. Without putting in this self-care work, you will burn out and your personal and professional lives will suffer for it. If the card is reversed, you have missed your moment to rest. The result is burnout and all the challenges that come with lack of sleep: lowered immunity, lowered sex drive, and irritability. Pulling this card reversed is a very strong warning to take a break now.

Upright Meaning:
Peacefulness, rejuvenation through rest, contemplation, solitude.

Reversed Meaning:
Burnt out, exhaustion due to refusal to rest, a need for recovery.

IT'S TIME FOR YOU TO SECLUDE YOURSELF, MEDITATE, SLEEP, AND GET BACK IN TOUCH WITH YOUR INNER SELF.

THE BITTERS BOUNTY

Have the cards foretold of a fight on the horizon, either within yourself or with someone else? The Bitters Bounty cocktail symbolizes this dispute, with its combating but complementary flavors. It is bright and herbal, yet spicy and bitter at the same time. With a bit of patience, it reaches harmony as the flavors meld together. Keep this message of poise and happy outcomes in mind as you decide how to proceed in your disagreement.

Add all ingredients to a cocktail shaker filled with ice. Shake, and strain into a coupe glass.

SERVES 1

1 ounce Angostura bitters

1 ounce orgeat

¾ ounce lime juice

¾ ounce Ancho Reyes liqueur

FIVE OF SWORDS

Pulling the Five of Swords is a warning that you will win a battle but lose valuable relationships in the process. You may have said or done hurtful things that alienated loved ones. Whatever it was, the Five of Swords appears to hold a mirror up to you regarding your actions and encourage you to make amends, apologize, and do better next time. If reversed, the Five of Swords is a pat on the back for your recent actions. You've either apologized or reconciled after a fight. You've taken responsibility, and that's not easy.

Upright Meaning:
Anxiety, depression, combativeness.

Reversed Meaning:
Atonement, apologetic, healing.

THE SWORDS' DISTRACTION

The Swords' Distraction is a tropical blend crafted to transport you elsewhere for a brief moment. The card indicates a time of calm after battle with the Five of Swords: Let the exciting green hue of the Midori and the tropical flavor profile remind you how sweet life can be when you remove yourself from toxic situations. Use this as an inspiration to achieve stability after a difficult experience.

1. Add all ingredients except pineapple wedge to a cocktail shaker. Dry shake.

2. Strain cocktail over Collins glass full of pebble ice. Garnish with skewered pineapple wedge on rim of glass.

SERVES 1

1½ ounces cachaça

¾ ounce Midori

½ ounce cognac-based orange liqueur

½ ounce lime juice

½ ounce pineapple juice

½ ounce Velvet Falernum

¼ ounce orgeat

1 grilled pineapple wedge

SIX OF SWORDS

The Six of Swords can be interpreted as being a little scary because it's about leaving your comfort zone, but when you see escapism portrayed in this card, it is a positive thing. You are being encouraged to leave a situation that is not healthy or is simply no longer serving you. If reversed, the Six of Wands is a sign that you are resisting the need to change. Start planning your way out.

Upright Meaning:
A time to rest after a fight, escaping a bad situation, maturing, achieving stability.

Reversed Meaning:
Stagnant or trapped, resistant to change or travel, slow progress.

THE DECEPTION

Like the Seven of Swords, The Deception is not what it seems. However, it is a welcome surprise in contrast to the thief depicted in its tarot muse. Appearing dark and strong but tasting sweet with hints of earthiness, this is a cocktail worth taking a chance on, unlike the person the Seven of Swords represents when upright.

———————◆———————

1. Add all ingredients except orange wheel to a mixing glass with ice. Stir, and strain into a coupe glass.

2. Float orange wheel on top for garnish.

SERVES 1

1½ ounces Amaro Sfumato

¾ ounce Amaro Nonino

2 dashes orange bitters

1 Candied Orange Wheel (see recipe in Chapter 3)

SEVEN OF SWORDS

The Seven of Swords is a trickster card, a warning about a fox in the henhouse, so to speak. If you pull this card upright, you or someone you know is aiming to deceive someone for profit. If this card is reversed, you or someone who has deceived you may be feeling a sense of guilt and a need to confess and apologize.

Upright Meaning:
Theft, deception, liar.

———◆———

Reversed Meaning:
Honesty, confessing, developing a conscious, feeling guilt.

YOU OR SOMEONE WHO HAS DECEIVED YOU
MAY BE FEELING A SENSE OF GUILT AND
A NEED TO CONFESS AND APOLOGIZE.

A BLINDING LIGHT

Are your hands tied when it comes to a certain situation? Having difficulty seeing through this moment? Like the Eight of Swords, A Blinding Light is dense, and you will be unable to see through it. The whiskey has a rich flavor, the espresso liqueur offers hints of bitterness, and the orange liqueur provides a bright light at the end of the tunnel. It serves as a flavorful reminder that there is still brightness in even the darkest situations.

1. Add all ingredients except espresso beans to a cocktail shaker filled with ice. Shake vigorously.

2. Strain into a rocks glass. Float espresso beans on top for garnish.

SERVES 1

1½ ounces applejack whiskey

1 ounce sweetened condensed milk

½ ounce Caffè Borghetti Espresso Liqueur

¼ ounce cognac-based orange liqueur

3 espresso beans

EIGHT OF SWORDS

The Eight of Swords signifies a time of helplessness when upright. Your hands are tied, and/or you are having difficulty seeing what the best path is to take. Everything feels like it's falling down on you, and you've lost control. Reversed, the Eight of Swords is about overcoming such challenges, which isn't easy either. Work to see yourself through to the other side.

Upright Meaning:
Loss of control, hands tied, difficulty navigating a situation.

Reversed Meaning:
Freedom, facing fears, empowerment and breaking free of constraints.

THE NEW NIGHTMARE

A variation on the Blood and Sand cocktail, The New Nightmare embodies the weighty message of the Nine of Swords. It blends Japanese whiskey with sweet vermouth and Cherry Heering, representing the darkness of depression, with hints of brightness in the orange juice to remind you that help is out there if only you ask. Muse over the support systems that are within reach as you combine and pour the ingredients of this complex potion.

---

1. Add all ingredients except orange wedge to a cocktail shaker filled with ice and shake, then strain into a martini glass.

2. Garnish with orange on rim of glass.

SERVES 1

¾ ounce Japanese whiskey

¾ ounce Velvet Falernum

¾ ounce sweet vermouth

¾ ounce pulp-free orange juice

½ ounce Cherry Heering

1 orange wedge slice, scored

NINE OF SWORDS

The Nine of Swords is about the anxieties and depressions in the world. This is a card of insomnia and loss of hope. Reversed, the Nine of Swords foretells asking for and receiving help. In the end, the Nine of Swords in either position is a reminder that everyone needs help sometimes. Ask, and you shall receive.

Upright Meaning:
Anxiety, depression, nightmares.

Reversed Meaning:
Letting go of anxieties, asking for help, moving on.

THE LAST CALL

Soothe the heavy message of the Ten of Swords with The Last Call. This crisp shot will encourage you to lay down difficult feelings, even just for a moment. You aren't ignoring them forever; you're simply taking a deserved rest. Bottoms up on this strong, simple libation; you can top it with soda water and sip, if you prefer that to a shot.

SERVES 1

1 ounce reposado tequila

1 ounce mezcal

1 dash lime juice

4 ounces seltzer water (optional)

1. Add tequila, mezcal, and lime juice to a rocks glass. Stir lightly.
2. Fill glass with ice. Top with seltzer water, if desired.

TEN OF SWORDS

The Ten of Swords warns of backstabbing and drama, but it can also signify the relief of hitting rock bottom. Upright, this is the beginning of your troubles. A failure of some kind may be in the future. Think of the upright interpretation as the beginning of a fall, whereas the reversed position signifies that you have stopped falling. Yes, you're at the bottom, but there is nowhere to go but up.

Upright Meaning:
Failure, exhaustion, giving up, backstabbing, drama.

Reversed Meaning:
Healing, hitting rock bottom and recovering, improvement.

CURIOUSER AND CURIOUSER

The Curiouser and Curiouser has roots in elixir flavors, offering "the medicine" to get you motivated in pursuing the new growth of the Page of Swords. Hibiscus is featured to improve overall well-being, and Green Chartreuse, a special potion made by French monks, offers all its herbal healing magic as well. Sip, and allow your curiosity to flourish.

1. Fill a king cube mold halfway with water. Add star anise, and allow to freeze about 4 hours. Fill remaining mold with water and freeze 6 hours.

2. Place star anise cube in a rocks glass.

3. Add remaining ingredients to a mixing glass with ice. Stir, and strain over star anise cube in glass.

SERVES 1

1 whole star anise pod

2 ounces cold dry white wine (pinot grigio recommended)

1½ ounces Lillet Blanc

½ ounce Green Chartreuse

½ ounce Hibiscus Syrup (see recipe in Chapter 3)

⅛ ounce pastis

1 king cube

PAGE OF SWORDS

The Page of Swords is new potential inspired by a fresh sense of curiosity. If you have been considering a new hobby or new venture, this Page has arrived to tell you to go for it. Overall, it's a good time for you to start something new from whatever it is that's made you curious. This curiosity has a lot of potential, so follow your instincts. If this card appears reversed, question what is holding you back and why. It is likely simply fear of failure.

Upright Meaning:
Self-expression, curiosity and growth, new potential.

Reversed Meaning:
No follow-through, being held back by fear of failure, no action or hasty action.

THE QUICK DRAW

The Knight of Swords is a person of action and speed, and for this reason, The Quick Draw is a variation of the classic revolver cocktail. This warm libation means well, like the Knight of Swords, and with the combination of espresso liqueur and bourbon, it goes down easy…maybe a little too easy?

1. Add all ingredients except orange swath to a mixing glass with ice. Stir, and strain into a coupe glass.
2. Flame orange swath and express over cocktail. Discard.

SERVES 1

2 ounces bourbon

½ ounce espresso liqueur

½ ounce Simple Syrup
(see recipe in Chapter 3)

¼ ounce cognac-based
orange liqueur

1 barspoon maraschino
cherry syrup

1 orange swath

KNIGHT OF SWORDS

The Knight of Swords means well and acts fast, but that often requires taking action before they have all the information or the valuable wisdom of a tarot Queen or King. This Knight is loyal like the other Knights in the Minor Arcana, with the intention and ability to be a problem-solver. When reversed, that vigor can easily turn to anger, violence, and confrontation. This isn't where you want to be emotionally, with no control over your anger.

Upright Meaning:
Fast action, knowledge but not wisdom, haste, problem-solver.

Reversed Meaning:
Argumentative, confrontational, violent, anger.

THE KNIGHT OF SWORDS MEANS WELL AND ACTS FAST, BUT THAT OFTEN REQUIRES TAKING ACTION BEFORE THEY HAVE ALL THE INFORMATION OR THE VALUABLE WISDOM OF A TAROT QUEEN OR KING.

MARIPOSA

The Queen of Swords sits on a throne engraved with butterflies. In an eye-catching tribute, the Mariposa (meaning "butterfly" in Spanish) uses butterfly blossom pea gin, giving it a gorgeous purple hue fit for a Queen. Enjoy this light tipple and reflect on the transformative power of the Queen of Swords.

———— ◆ ————

1. Add all ingredients except flower to shaker filled with ice. Shake, and strain into a coupe glass.

2. Float flower on top for garnish.

SERVES 1

1 ounce Empress 1908 Gin

3/4 ounce Cardamaro

3/4 ounce grapefruit juice

1/2 ounce pamplemousse liqueur

1 edible purple flower (violet or pansy)

QUEEN OF SWORDS

The Queen of Swords is educated, wise, and, most importantly, receptive to the opinions of others. They remain informed with their openness and are looked to for advice and decision-making. This Queen is highly perceptive and able to communicate directly and effectively. When reversed, this Queen is quite the opposite and difficult to be around. They can be cold and downright mean, and lack adequate communication skills.

Upright Meaning:
Honesty, someone with principles, boundaries, direct and clear communication with others.

———— ◆ ————

Reversed Meaning:
No emotional balance, reactive and cold, passive-aggressive.

THE PAPILLON

Like the Queen of Swords, the King of Swords' throne is engraved with butterflies. For this reason, The Papillon (meaning "butterfly" in French) features butterfly pea blossom to give the cocktail a royal shade of purple. Butterfly pea flowers are protective, attract love, and even enhance memory and cognitive function. The Swords suit of tarot, being air signs, are tied to the conscious mind, making the iconic purple of butterfly pea blossoms even more perfect for this ode to the King.

1. Fill a king cube mold halfway with water. Add flower, and allow to freeze about 4 hours. Fill remaining mold with water and freeze 6 hours.

2. Place cube in a rocks glass.

3. Add remaining ingredients to a mixing glass with ice. Stir, and strain over king cube in glass.

SERVES 1

1 edible purple flower (violet or pansy)

1½ ounces Empress 1908 Gin

¾ ounce pamplemousse liqueur

¼ ounce elderflower liqueur

1 king cube

KING OF SWORDS

The King of Swords is an authoritative leader. They are wise, with a strong control of their higher consciousness. They are also self-disciplined and likely self-made. This is a person to look up to. If the cards indicate that this is you, this is a good person to be. If reversed, the King is cruel and abusive, so take heed and reflect on your actions if the reversed King of Swords is pointing to you.

Upright Meaning:
Ethical, having integrity, a good sense of self-discipline, authoritative.

Reversed Meaning:
Cruel, oppressive, verbally abusive.

CHAPTER 8

THE MAJOR ARCANA RECIPES

THE FOOL'S ERRAND

A divinely inspired spin on the Bee's Knees, this cocktail features a familiar blend of flavors with hints of new elements from the rose water and egg white. Roses are used to attract love and friendship in spellwork, and their presence in this recipe represents the hopeful future for meaningful relationships ahead. The bee pollen garnish is a symbol of pollinating something new with the possibility of growth and beauty. The Fool's Errand is as full of potential as the person sipping it.

1. Add all ingredients except bee pollen into a cocktail shaker. Dry shake 1 minute. Add ice and shake another 2 minutes.

2. Strain into a Nick and Nora glass. Float bee pollen balls on top for garnish.

SERVES 1

2 ounces gin

¾ ounce lemon juice

¾ ounce Honey Syrup (see recipe in Chapter 3)

3 dashes rose water

1 large egg white

¼ teaspoon bee pollen balls

THE FOOL.

THE FOOL

The Fool represents a delicate time of starting something new. While The Fool may look like they don't know what they're doing, remember that they appear in the Major Arcana and therefore have the wealth of experience in smaller life changes behind them. The Fool is therefore confident and optimistic, and that brings both successes and failures. Reversed, The Fool is reckless. Stop and think about what you're doing and what the consequences could be. Chances are, it's not worth the risk.

Upright Meaning:
A new phase in life, childlike innocence, leaping into something new and unknown.

Reversed Meaning:
A reckless or poorly conceived risk, leaping without looking, thoughtlessness.

THE MAGICIAN'S CREATION

The cocktail for The Magician must be equally as magical and steadfast as this card, which is why its roots are in the classic Sazerac, the mother of all cocktails. The simple balance of aged rum with sweet and bitter flavors makes the basis of something delicious and transformative. Enjoy this cocktail and remember that it is only the beginning of your transformation.

1. Add sugar cube and water to a rocks glass. Muddle until sugar begins to dissolve.

2. Add rum and stir until sugar is completely dissolved.

3. Add king cube. Express lemon swath over cocktail and discard.

SERVES 1

1 Homemade Peychaud's Bitters Sugar Cube (see recipe in Chapter 3)

½ ounce chilled filtered water

2 ounces aged rum

1 king cube

1 lemon swath

THE MAGICIAN

The Magician involves all four suits of the Minor Arcana. This card therefore masters and balances all four elements of earth, air, fire, and water. The Magician works with all suits and elements as they transform and create. It is a great sign for a creative project or a big change you're considering. Reversed, it is a sign to take heed of friends around you. If someone seems to be deceitful or too good to be true, they probably are.

Upright Meaning:
Action, transformation, magic, intellect.

Reversed Meaning:
Not magic but trickery, deception, a con, someone to keep at an arm's length.

THE MAGICIAN WORKS WITH ALL SUITS AND ELEMENTS AS THEY TRANSFORM AND CREATE. IT IS A GREAT SIGN FOR A CREATIVE PROJECT OR A BIG CHANGE YOU'RE CONSIDERING.

THE IMMORTAL PRIESTESS

The High Priestess is about traditional ritual and religion, with roots in Judaism. As such, The Immortal Priestess uses Bernheim bourbon, which was named for one of the fathers of American whiskey, a Jewish immigrant from Germany. This cocktail also features pomegranate, a symbol of resurrection and immortality (and a fruit that is featured prominently in many of the Rider–Waite tarot cards). Like its divine inspiration, The Immortal Priestess encompasses ritual, immortality, and tradition.

1. Fill a round king cube mold halfway with water. Add flower, and allow to freeze about 4 hours. Fill remaining mold with water and freeze 6 hours.

2. Place round ice with flower in a goblet or large red wine glass.

3. Add remaining ingredients to a cocktail shaker filled with ice and shake. Strain over ice into glass.

SERVES 1

1 edible flower in color of choice

¾ ounce Bernheim bourbon

¾ ounce PAMA Pomegranate Liqueur

¾ ounce Simple Syrup (see recipe in Chapter 3)

½ ounce lemon juice

½ ounce lime juice

1 barspoon date syrup

1 round king cube

THE HIGH PRIESTESS

The High Priestess represents strong feminine energy, immortality, and sacred knowledge. This card shows a confident and competent person with a strong female spirit. Pulling this card is a message to get in touch with your spiritual side and the rituals of your ancestors. When reversed, The High Priestess is telling you that you need to respect the religion of your ancestors and possibly even learn their ways. You have a blockage in your spirituality and emotions, and respecting the ways of your ancestors is a good way to remove that blockage.

Upright Meaning:
Traditional magic, wisdom, power, sacred knowledge, spirituality.

Reversed Meaning:
An emotional blockage, a sacred disconnect, not respecting the old ways.

APHRODITE'S BLESSINGS

The Empress is the divine feminine, connected to nature and love, so it is only fitting that the cocktail crafted in their honor is inspired by Aphrodite, the goddess of love. Aphrodite's Blessings is all about seduction and decadence, represented by the chocolate and orange flavors. Chocolate is an aphrodisiac, eliciting seduction. Oranges are uplifting magical fruits that are used to represent abundance. So, sit back and enjoy your abundance and your sensuality with Aphrodite's Blessings.

1. Add all ingredients except chocolate syrup and orange wheel to a mixing glass with ice. Stir, and strain into a coupe glass.

2. Gently pour chocolate syrup into middle of glass so that it settles on the bottom for garnish. Skewer orange wheel through pith on both sides and balance across rim.

SERVES 1

1½ ounces bourbon

1 ounce crème de cacao

½ ounce cognac-based orange liqueur

⅛ ounce chocolate syrup

1 Candied Orange Wheel (see recipe in Chapter 3)

THE EMPRESS

The Empress is a mature, confident person with a strong connection to nature and creativity. This card is the "yes" you need if you are considering starting a family, new business venture, or new creative endeavor. The Empress is harmonious with nature, secure in themselves, and has a solid foundation of emotional, fiscal, mental, and sexual health. Reversed, The Empress is overindulgent with no self-confidence. They are emotionally immature and difficult to be around, as they tend to stir up drama.

Upright Meaning:
The divine feminine, seduction, sensual, fertile, loving, self-confidence, self-love.

Reversed Meaning:
Insecure, overindulgent, immature, self-conscious.

THE "YES" YOU NEED IF YOU ARE
CONSIDERING STARTING A FAMILY,
NEW BUSINESS VENTURE, OR
NEW CREATIVE ENDEAVOR.

THE EMPEROR'S CEREBRAL ENERGY

The purple hue of this cocktail represents royalty and the regal authority of The Emperor card. And with such indulgent flavors as blueberry and Amaretto, it is the perfect ode to this tarot archetype. Blueberries are known to increase focus and mental stamina, two things The Emperor possesses in abundance. The Emperor's Cerebral Energy is fit for celebrating anyone with focus, authority, and decadence, or for encouraging more of The Emperor's intellectual and assertive energy in your life.

1. Add all ingredients except tincture and blueberries to a cocktail shaker filled with ice. Shake, and pour with dirty rocks into a wine goblet.

2. Top with Butterfly Pea Flower Tincture, pouring slowly to create a top layer.

3. Garnish with skewered blueberries. Stir before enjoying or sip with a straw.

SERVES 1

1 ounce white rum

1 ounce aged rum

1 ounce Blueberry Syrup (see recipe in Chapter 3)

3/4 ounce lime juice

1/2 ounce lemon juice

1/2 ounce Velvet Falernum

1 barspoon Amaretto

1/2 ounce Butterfly Pea Flower Tincture (see recipe in Chapter 3)

3 fresh blueberries

THE EMPEROR

The Emperor is a strong figure who has control over others. They exude a fierce masculine energy and protect their emotions with their armor. For those reasons, emotions are not a huge factor with The Emperor: They are all about the mind. They can become domineering and too controlling when reversed, but when upright, they are a positive, strong patriarch.

Upright Meaning:
Authority, focus, determination, masculine energy.

Reversed Meaning:
Domineering, overbearing, inflexible, lack of authority.

THE WISE ONE

The Hierophant is a wise authority figure, which is why this cocktail is inspired by the classic old fashioned. The Wise One is rich and balanced, like The Hierophant, but its roots are also literally old fashioned. And while understanding the old traditions is important, so is growth in new directions. The Cherry Heering offers a deep fruit flavor, and cherries represent youth and fertility, two things The Hierophant should take heed from. The Wise One is a unique mixture of traditional and novel.

1. Add everything except orange swath and king cube to a mixing glass with ice. Stir, and strain over king cube in a rocks glass.

2. Flame orange swath over glass and discard.

SERVES 1

1½ ounces bourbon

½ ounce Chai Syrup
(see recipe in Chapter 3)

½ ounce Cherry Heering

1 orange swath

1 round king cube

THE HIEROPHANT

The Hierophant is an authoritative figure who knows the laws and rules and lives strictly by them. This person believes strongly in what is tried and true, and struggles with nonconformists and breaking any rules. Pulling this card could indicate legal trouble, for example, but it could also indicate help from a rule follower in your life, depending on the card spread and where this card lies. Reversed, this card could be pointing you to take a less-traveled path and rebel against traditions in your family or culture that are holding you back.

Upright Meaning:
Educated, wise, knowledgeable, an authority figure in traditional ways, a conformist and conservative person.

Reversed Meaning:
Rebel, unconventional way of living, poor leadership, challenging traditional ways.

THIS CARD COULD BE POINTING YOU TO TAKE A LESS-TRAVELED PATH AND REBEL AGAINST TRADITIONS IN YOUR FAMILY OR CULTURE THAT ARE HOLDING YOU BACK.

ORIGINAL SIN

As the tarot has indicated, two souls have come together. In this case, those souls are the fruity, bright flavors of orange and apple, with the richness of whiskey and maple syrup. Original Sin is made with applejack whiskey to represent the apple that Eve gave to Adam in the biblical tale. The maple syrup represents the tree of knowledge and the leaves with which Adam and Eve covered themselves. Oranges are used in spells for abundance, further tying this cocktail to the elements of abundant joy and unification. Original Sin is a decadent reminder that knowledge is delicious and so are healthy partnerships.

1. Add all ingredients except orange swath to a rocks glass. Stir.
2. Express orange swath over glass, rub it along rim, and discard.

SERVES 1

2 ounces applejack whiskey

¼ ounce pure maple syrup

½ ounce filtered water

2 dashes Angostura bitters

1 dash orange bitters

1 barspoon Amaro Nonino

1 king cube

1 orange swath

THE LOVERS

The Lovers appears upright to tell of an upcoming union. The relationship is healthy, with honesty and open communication. It could be romantic, professional, or platonic. When reversed, this card still refers to relationships, but there is an imbalance or lack of clarity in a relationship. The intimacy is real and worth fighting for, though, so don't necessarily walk away if The Lovers is reversed. Balance is necessary in any relationship; it's time to take inventory of yours.

Upright Meaning:
A meaningful connection, a unity of souls, honest communication.

Reversed Meaning:
Lack of communication, disharmony, a relationship imbalance.

THE JOURNEY

The Chariot is all about leaving your comfort zone and racing into action, and for that reason, the cocktail crafted in its honor is inspired by the classic Sidecar—named for enjoying the ride. When you first pour this concoction, you will see a layer between the blue of the body of the recipe and the red of the sunken grenadine. These layers represent steps in a journey, and while mixing them makes the drink murky, not knowing what's on the other side of your adventure is half the fun.

1. Add all ingredients except grenadine to a cocktail shaker filled with ice. Shake, and strain into a martini glass.

2. Carefully drop grenadine into glass to create a layer on the bottom. Stir before enjoying.

SERVES 1

2 ounces brandy

¾ ounce orgeat

½ ounce blue curaçao

½ ounce lemon juice

¼ ounce grenadine

THE CHARIOT

The Chariot appears in a reading to tell you that the time to act is now—not only because it's the right moment but also because you are in a great position to succeed in your next endeavor. This is a big journey, unlike the ones represented by the Knights in the Minor Arcana. The Chariot's adventure won't be easy, but it will be worth every step. Reversed, The Chariot is a call to get yourself focused and moving. You have become complacent when you should be more ambitious. Movement feels scary, especially when things are shaky to begin with, but pulling The Chariot is a call forward, reversed or not.

Upright Meaning:
The ability to succeed, arduous tasks ahead, you are on the right path.

Reversed Meaning:
No direction or stability, a call to get organized and focus on movement forward, stagnation.

THE WARRIOR'S MANHATTAN

There is great power within you, and The Warrior's Manhattan was designed to remind you of this fact. Its roots are in the classic Manhattan, using Luxardo Bitter Bianco rather than the smoothness of sweet vermouth to wake up your palate. This cocktail is as fearless as you must be, full of strong ingredients ready to illustrate what they are each capable of. Take a note from The Warrior's Manhattan and show the world what you're made of.

1. Add all ingredients except lemon swath to a mixing glass with ice. Stir, and strain into a Manhattan glass.

2. Express lemon swath over drink, and drop in for garnish.

SERVES 1

2 ounces bourbon

1 ounce Luxardo Bitter Bianco

2 dashes sarsaparilla bitters

1 lemon swath

STRENGTH

The Strength card, whether upright or reversed, is reminding you of the strength and abilities within you. While the upright position means you are more assured in your inner strength, pulling this card reversed is telling you that you're stronger than you think. Both readings are positive because all the power already resides in you. This is overall a wonderful card to pull, no matter where or how it falls in your reading.

Upright Meaning:
Fearless, gentle resistance, inner strength.

Reversed Meaning:
Loss of confidence, a need to find your inner strength again, facing a failure.

THE PATH WALKED ALONE

Are you faced with a spiritual and emotional journey that you must go on alone? The Path Walked Alone is crafted with lavender to help calm and focus your mind, and honey to rest and soothe your mind and body, so you are ready to take the next step. Lavender has been used in spellwork for centuries to relax and induce sleep. Honey is a medicinal, soothing syrup. This herbal and bright cocktail goes down easy, readying you for meditation and inner focus.

1. Add all ingredients except orange wheel to a cocktail shaker filled with ice. Strain into a rocks glass.

2. Float orange wheel on top for garnish.

SERVES 1

1½ ounces Carpano Botanic

¾ ounce lemon juice

¾ ounce Lavender Honey Syrup (see recipe in Chapter 3)

1 orange wheel

THE HERMIT

The Hermit card appears to tell you that it's time to separate from the group and spend time with yourself to gain inner wisdom. The Hermit is the introvert in everyone and demands time to recharge, reflect, and come out stronger. If reversed, this card is telling you that you've done this too much and it's time to rejoin the group. This card could also be reminding you that if you feel stuck in a rut and are lonely, you should ask for help from loved ones. The Hermit has helped many, and there are multitudes of people who would be happy to help The Hermit in return.

Upright Meaning:
A need for spiritual and emotional healing, a need to be apart from others to grow personally, inner wisdom.

Reversed Meaning:
Loneliness, pushing others away too often or too much, a reminder to ask for support from others.

THE GOLDEN PINEAPPLE

The Wheel of Fortune is about luck, health, and happiness. Fittingly, The Golden Pineapple features a traditional fruit of luck: the pineapple. Blending sweet flavors, The Golden Pineapple is smooth, bright, and exciting. It is meant to remind you that life is good, and you are fortunate in your circumstances. Cheers to your blessings, and may many more come soon.

———————•◆•———————

1. Add all ingredients except pineapple wedge to a cocktail shaker filled with ice. Shake, and strain into a coupe glass.

2. Garnish with pineapple wedge on rim.

SERVES 1

1½ ounces Amaro Averna

¾ ounce pineapple juice

½ ounce Honey Syrup (see recipe in Chapter 3)

¼ ounce lime juice

1 small pineapple wedge, scored

WHEEL OF FORTUNE

All of our lives rotate through new beginnings, which often means ending old relationships, routines, or locations. Pulling the Wheel of Fortune is telling you a change like this is ahead, and while it might be painful, it will be positive in the long run. This card is also strongly tied to karma, so you will be seeing either positive or negative results of your actions depending on if this card is upright or reversed. If the Wheel of Fortune is reversed, it is telling you of difficulty up ahead. This means you will find a necessary change nearly impossible to make, or you will find yourself feeling caught in the same, unfulfilling loop. If you're having thoughts about a drastic life change and the Wheel of Fortune appears reversed to you, consider what's holding you back and why.

Upright Meaning:
A good fortune card, a big change ahead, fate, the end of something old and beginning of something new, the karmic circle.

———————•◆•———————

Reversed Meaning:
Poor luck ahead, negative changes or stagnation, difficulties in making changes, no control.

ALL OF OUR LIVES ROTATE THROUGH
NEW BEGINNINGS, WHICH OFTEN MEANS
ENDING OLD RELATIONSHIPS,
ROUTINES, OR LOCATIONS.

KARMIC FRUIT

Is justice at the front of your thoughts? Perhaps the tarot has brought it to your attention? There are consequences to all actions, and Karmic Fruit proves to be a delicious reminder of this. The Carpano Antica of this cocktail brings deep cherry notes to the nutty Amaretto base. Its richness and fruit-of-the-earth flavor profile elicit the rewarding sense of karmic fruit. As you collect, shake, and pour the ingredients, remember that you reap what you sow.

1. Add all ingredients except pecans to a cocktail shaker. Dry shake 1 minute. Add ice and shake 2 more minutes.

2. Strain into a coupe glass. Sprinkle with crushed pecans for garnish.

SERVES 1

1½ ounces **Amaretto**

1 ounce **Carpano Antica**

½ ounce **lemon juice**

½ ounce **Simple Syrup** (see recipe in Chapter 3)

1 large **egg white**

¼ teaspoon **crushed pecans**

JUSTICE

The Justice card is about balance and karma. Everything that you have put into the subject of your reading, whether it be love, career, or spiritual growth, will begin to cycle back to either reward or punish you. If you have not given something enough energy or the right kind of energy, you won't see the results you wanted. Justice, like karma, does not lie. Reversed, the Justice card is not bad karma; rather, it signifies negative energies of dishonesty and corruption. It is a call about someone near you who is out of balance and taking more than they have earned or deserve.

Upright Meaning:
Cause and effect, karma, truth, balance.

Reversed Meaning:
Unfairness, dishonesty, corruption, avoidance.

DO OR DIE

Intentional pauses can be just as important as the actions you take. Like The Hanged Man in tarot, Do or Die reminds you to take an intentional pause and practice patience when crafting something beautiful—as the monks who craft the Green Chartreuse in this drink do. Strawberries are a survival fruit that represent growth against all odds, a sweet message that you can thrive in unlikely situations. Enjoy Do or Die and remember that patience is key, but don't stall on decisions either.

---

1. Add all ingredients except strawberry slice to a cocktail shaker filled with ice. Shake, and strain into a Manhattan glass.

2. Garnish with strawberry slice on rim.

SERVES 1

1½ ounces bourbon

¾ ounce Quick Strawberry Shrub (see recipe in Chapter 3)

½ ounce lime juice

¼ ounce Green Chartreuse

1 fresh strawberry slice, scored

THE HANGED MAN

The Hanged Man is about giving in to the universe for a moment. Taking a break or getting an unexpected quiet time away from work can be very healthy for your mind and body. Let yourself unwind with some downtime. The Hanged Man also encourages patience and trusting the process. If reversed, The Hanged Man has been hanging too long. They are stuck in their ways, stubborn, and therefore have stopped growing. They could also be telling you that you need a break that you aren't giving yourself.

Upright Meaning:
A pause in your life, stagnation, a time to embrace the stillness, patience.

Reversed Meaning:
Needing a pause that you aren't taking, a call to see things from another perspective, stuck in your ways and resistant to change, stubbornness.

TAKING A BREAK OR GETTING
AN UNEXPECTED QUIET TIME AWAY
FROM WORK CAN BE VERY HEALTHY FOR
YOUR MIND AND BODY.

DEATH IS THE BEGINNING

It's only fitting that the cocktail that embodies the Death card in tarot is a play on the classic Death in the Afternoon. Sip this simple and strong blend of absinthe and champagne as you consider what the tarot may be telling you to shed for new growth—perhaps even a brand-new beginning—to occur.

1. Add sugar cube to a champagne flute, then top with absinthe. Slowly add champagne to fill.

2. Express lemon swath over drink and discard.

SERVES 1

1 Homemade Peychaud's Bitters Sugar Cube (see recipe in Chapter 3)

½ ounce absinthe

3 ounces champagne

1 lemon swath

DEATH

The Death card might be scary to see, but it is really a sign that you are shedding an old version of yourself or some part of your life that no longer serves you. Like a snake shedding its skin, you have outgrown something. If the Death card is upright, you are on a healthy path for growth. If the Death card is reversed, that energy is blocked. You are resisting the change due to fear and stubbornness. Remember that change is a natural part of life, as is death itself.

Upright Meaning:
Shedding ways that no longer serve you, personal growth, outgrowing your old life or relationships, renewal, transitions.

Reversed Meaning:
Fear of change, too stubborn to change, making the same mistakes repeatedly.

ELIXIR OF LIFE

Temperance is a medicinal card about tranquility and harmony. For this reason, the Elixir of Life uses Becherovka, a cinnamon and orangey spirit from the Czech Republic with a closely guarded recipe. With over a hundred herbs involved in the creation of Becherovka, there is no shortage of flavor and magical properties coming from this tasty liqueur. The addition of Orange Syrup and a Candied Orange Wheel brings the energizing and prosperity magic of oranges and brightens this delicious toddy. Enjoy this herb-packed potion and focus on harmonizing with the universe.

SERVES 1

1½ ounces Becherovka

½ ounce Orange Syrup
(see recipe in Chapter 3)

6 ounces hot water

1 Candied Orange Wheel
(see recipe in Chapter 3)

1. Add Becherovka and Orange Syrup to a toddy mug. Top with hot water.
2. Skewer orange wheel through pith. Garnish mug with skewer resting across the rim.

TEMPERANCE

Temperance is about being in balance with your various responsibilities, loved ones, and the universe. Having it appear upright is a great sign for the work you put in to achieve this difficult life balance. Pulling Temperance reversed indicates a severe lack of balance due to overindulgence. Furthermore, this card points out that any dissatisfaction in your life right now is a direct result of your actions. Change is possible, but you're the only one that can do it for yourself.

Upright Meaning:
Balance, tranquility, harmony, serenity, calmness.

Reversed Meaning:
Lack of balance in your life leading to unease, overindulgence, addiction.

CHANGE IS POSSIBLE,
BUT YOU'RE THE ONLY ONE THAT
CAN DO IT FOR YOURSELF.

THE TEMPTATION

Illustrating the addiction and harmful habits indicated by The Devil, The Temptation uses smoke to represent the tempting lure of a common, addictive vice. And true to life's temptations, this cocktail is quite enjoyable. Enjoy this smoky tipple as you consider what vices or habits may be negatively affecting your life.

Add all ingredients to a mixing glass with ice. Stir, and strain into a coupe glass.

SERVES 1

1½ ounces mezcal

¾ ounce Amaro Averna

½ ounce Fernet-Branca

½ ounce Simple Syrup
(see recipe in Chapter 3)

½ barspoon activated charcoal

THE DEVIL

The Devil holds up a mirror to our flaws and negative habits. They could be pointing to a vice of yours that has become an addiction, or to a toxic relationship you need to get out of. Whatever it is, The Devil appears to tell you to get out or face destruction. If reversed, The Devil is condoning the work you've put in to break bad habits or fight addiction. Your journey is not complete, but you're almost there.

Upright Meaning:
Addictions, harmful cycles, vices, destructive behavior.

Reversed Meaning:
Putting in the work to break bad habits, getting to the other side of destructive cycles, overcoming addictions.

THE FLAMING TOWER

Flaming like the imagery of The Tower, this cocktail burns with a message that it is time to move on from a current situation. The smokiness of the mezcal reflects the smoke that billows up to the sky on the card, while the flamed lime represents the fire that people are fleeing. If you were looking for a sign to leave a current situation, The Flaming Tower is it. The flavors are smoky and sweet, with hints of bitter, just like leaving a situation that no longer serves you: Parts of the exit will be bitter, but in the end, it's best to move on.

1. Add all ingredients except lime and rum to a cocktail shaker. Dry shake, and pour over ice in a Collins glass.
2. Float lime on top of drink, and fill with overproof rum.
3. Light rum on fire. Extinguish and remove lime before drinking.

SERVES 1

1½ ounces mezcal

¾ ounce grapefruit juice

¾ ounce Agave Syrup (see recipe in Chapter 3)

½ ounce pamplemousse liqueur

1 pinch salt

½ medium lime, hollowed out

½ ounce overproof rum

THE TOWER

The Tower is a sign that a large or sudden change is coming. While it will rock your world, it is a necessary change. Something very familiar to you is falling apart, and it will be jarring for a moment. However, the result of whatever event happens will be better for you in the long run, so do your best to trust the process. If you pull The Tower reversed, you are resisting the change that needs to happen. Whether you're turning a blind eye to the facts or flat-out refusing to change, you aren't helping anyone with this stubbornness.

> **Upright Meaning:**
> *Time to leave, a current state of falling apart, sudden but complete and necessary change.*
>
> **Reversed Meaning:**
> *Resisting necessary change, turning a blind eye to the need for change, believing your own lies.*

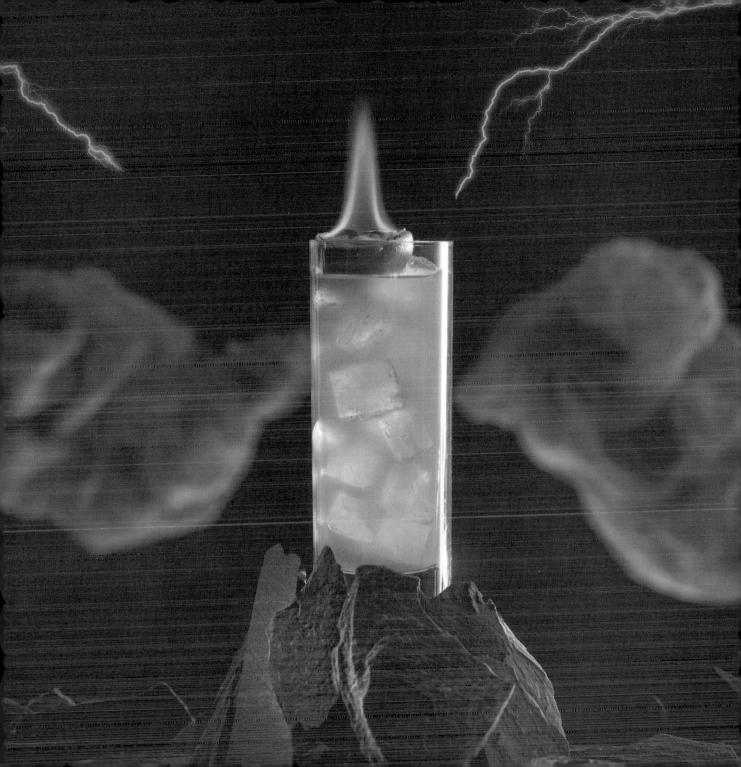

STARTINI

After a tumultuous time comes a period of healing and peace. The Startini is light and bright, like a star, with a starfruit garnish to remind you to keep your faith in the universe, however difficult things may have been recently. The kumquat flavors are your sweet treat for surviving the challenges life sends your way. The cocktail itself is clear but for the edible glitter, which shimmers like the stars, and you.

1. Add all ingredients except starfruit to a mixing glass with ice. Stir.
2. Strain into a martini glass. Garnish with skewered starfruit slice resting in glass.

SERVES 1

1½ ounces gin

½ ounce kumquat liqueur

½ ounce Starfruit Syrup (see recipe in Chapter 3)

1 barspoon cocktail glitter

1 slice fresh starfruit

THE STAR

Whether The Star is drawn upright or reversed, it indicates that you have just been through a very challenging time. Something that was solid has fallen around you. If The Star is upright, it means you are entering a peaceful time of healing and calmness. If The Star is reversed, the event that caused you stress has also caused a loss of hope. Depression and lack of ambition will follow. Take note from The Star upright and embrace the calm after the storm.

Upright Meaning:
Clarity, peace after a difficult time, calmness, a time to heal.

Reversed Meaning:
Loss of faith due to difficult times, loss of motivation, depression, loss of passion and creativity.

YOU HAVE JUST BEEN THROUGH
A VERY CHALLENGING TIME.
SOMETHING THAT WAS SOLID
HAS FALLEN AROUND YOU.

THE MOON'S SHINE

Are you feeling scared about moving forward, regardless of what you know to be necessary? The tropical flavor and bright color of The Moon's Shine will wake up your palate and give you that little push needed to keep journeying toward the juicy future you deserve. The Suze incorporates just a hint of bitterness to balance the drink, keeping you focused.

Add all ingredients to a mixing glass with ice. Stir, and strain into a coupe glass.

SERVES 1

1 ounce moonshine

½ ounce Midori

¼ ounce banana liqueur

¼ ounce Suze

1 barspoon cocktail glitter

THE MOON

The Moon is a mystical card that symbolizes fear and illusion. It asks the question: When the moon shines, what comes to light? The Moon represents a need for change or acknowledges a change that has already occurred. Therefore, whether it is upright or reversed, this is an optimistic card. It is all about confronting your fears and shining a light on any negativity lurking in the darkness. Something around you isn't quite what it seems, and it is time to figure out what that thing is.

Upright Meaning:
Reflection, controlling fear, trusting instincts.

Reversed Meaning:
Confrontation, ending toxic relationships, change.

HERE COMES THE SUN

In life and in tarot, The Sun is a bright burst of vitality-giving light. Here Comes the Sun is bright like the sun with all that fire energy to motivate you into the next stage of your life cycle. Its roots are in the tequila sunrise, heralding in a new day and fresh start. Pears symbolize divine sustenance, and the Pear Syrup in this recipe not only sweetens the potion; it also infuses it with the abundance and longevity of pear magic.

1. Add all ingredients except grenadine to a cocktail shaker filled with ice. Shake, and strain into a martini glass.

2. Gently pour grenadine into glass. It will settle on the bottom, creating a layer.

SERVES 1

1½ ounces reposado tequila

1 ounce pulp-free orange juice

½ ounce Pear Syrup (see recipe in Chapter 3)

½ ounce grenadine

THE SUN

No matter what spread you're working with, The Sun is a big indicator of a time of happiness, health, and fun. The Sun wants you to remember the blessings you have and focus on those things right now. If The Sun is reversed, you're finding this very difficult. Negativity, lack of energy, and general bitterness have made you give up. This slump is temporary, but you will have to put in the work to snap out of it. Take a cue from The Sun (in the upright position) and look on the bright side.

Upright Meaning:
Good health, new life, energy, warmth, fun, freedom.

Reversed Meaning:
No ambition, negative feelings, lack of energy, lazy.

REMEMBER THE BLESSINGS YOU HAVE
AND FOCUS ON THOSE THINGS
RIGHT NOW.

A NEW AGE

Big changes are ahead! You've survived turmoil and tests and now it's time to ready yourself for a fresh adventure. This is also a time to choose your next steps, and, for that reason, you can make this drink either a mocktail or cocktail. Inspired by the Cosmopolitan, A New Age uses hibiscus, which attracts love and lust and brings tartness to the flavor of the drink. Hibiscus magic adds fire and excitement to your next move, with or without the vodka, so add the spirit or leave it out—the judgment is yours.

1. Add all ingredients except flower to a cocktail shaker filled with ice. Shake, and strain into a coupe glass.

2. Float flower on top for garnish.

SERVES 1

1 ounce vodka (optional)

1 ounce Seedlip Grove 42 Nonalcoholic Spirits

¾ ounce Hibiscus Syrup (see recipe in Chapter 3)

½ ounce lime juice

1 edible pink flower (pansy or rose)

JUDGMENT

If you pull Judgment in a tarot reading, the next steps for you are from an inner calling. This means it's time to trust your intuition in making the decisions ahead of you. If Judgment is reversed in a reading, it is asking you to reflect and get in touch with your higher self to make the best choice. This could also indicate that you are your harshest critic and need to quiet that negative voice in your head telling you that you can't do something.

Upright Meaning:
Absolution, new beginning, big changes, intuitive decision making.

Reversed Meaning:
A time to meditate or reflect in order to make an intuitive decision, lack of confidence, being hard on yourself.

THE WORLD IS YOURS

This cocktail, like its tarot namesake, embodies all of humankind, as well as earth-dwelling animals, water animals, and animals of flight. The drink is colored green by matcha to represent the planet, with a frothy top of egg white to represent the air and a clear base spirit (white rum) to represent water. The World Is Yours has a bit of everything; it is love, harmony, and balance. It is your scrumptious reward for a job well done.

1. Add all ingredients except a pinch of matcha to a cocktail shaker and dry shake. Add ice and shake again.
2. Strain into a coupe glass.
3. Sprinkle remaining matcha on top for garnish.

SERVES 1

2 ounces white rum

¾ ounce Simple Syrup (see recipe in Chapter 3)

½ ounce Velvet Falernum

½ ounce lime juice

1 large egg white

1 barspoon sweet matcha, divided

THE WORLD

The World is a wonderful card to pull upright. It indicates that the cycle you're on will end successfully with full growth and closure. This means that the next step of your life will be off to a good start. You've put in the work and grown; you have learned and are ready to start over again as The Fool in your new life cycle. If The World is reversed, you are experiencing a blockage of all these successes. You haven't healed properly from the trauma of your past, and you aren't letting go or trusting your instincts. This behavior leads to stagnation. Trust the process and let yourself let go of the grudges, the hostility, and the pain. The next cycle will begin with or without you.

Upright Meaning:
Unity, completion, a successful completion of a life cycle.

Reversed Meaning:
Blockage, lack of success, no closure, disappointment, no movement.

TAROT CARD MEANINGS

The following is a quick reference for each tarot card. These keywords will help you decipher the cards' overall meanings when doing a reading or when looking for inspiration for your own cocktail recipes.

MINOR ARCANA

Ace of Wands
- Upright: Ambition, creative breakthrough, a fresh professional challenge
- Reversed: Self-imposed limits, laziness, bound by outdated constructs

Two of Wands
- Upright: Good decision(s), mental clarity, taking responsibility
- Reversed: Poor decisions, not thinking things through, fear of change

Three of Wands
- Upright: Opportunity to travel, professional headway, personal growth
- Reversed: Poor self-esteem, shame, self-restriction

Four of Wands
- Upright: Merriment, party, the beginning of more to celebrate
- Reversed: Argument with family or close friend, disharmony within you, loss of a relationship

Five of Wands

- **Upright:** Discord, argumentative, fighting
- **Reversed:** Taking the high road, apologizing, repairing broken relationships

Six of Wands

- **Upright:** Progress forward after disharmony, results of hard work, movement forward after struggles
- **Reversed:** Stagnation, regrets, unsuccessful endeavors

Seven of Wands

- **Upright:** Standing your ground, defending something you've created, self-reliance in a difficult time
- **Reversed:** Quitting, submitting, letting someone take what's yours

Eight of Wands

- **Upright:** Self-confidence, fast decisions, and quick follow-up actions
- **Reversed:** Impatient, acting without thinking, hesitating, and missing an opportunity

Nine of Wands

- **Upright:** Burned out, drained, weary due to overwork
- **Reversed:** Refusal to take time off, overtired, hardheaded

Ten of Wands

- **Upright:** Exhaustion, a need to take a rest, an acceptance of taking a break
- **Reversed:** Refusing to rest, burning out, losing grip because you refuse to take a break

Page of Wands

- **Upright:** New beginning, a nonconformist, inspiration
- **Reversed:** Fearful of changes, hindering due to fear, monotonous

Knight of Wands

- **Upright:** A daring person, free spirit, traveler, adventurer
- **Reversed:** Scared to change, refusal to travel, impatient, lack of confidence

Queen of Wands

- **Upright:** Fertility, female strength, sensual, determined
- **Reversed:** Submissive, unambitious, infertile, impotent, incapable

King of Wands

- **Upright:** Positive, masculine energy, leader, role model, businessperson
- **Reversed:** Domineering, egotistical, self-centered

Ace of Cups

- **Upright:** Emotional awakening, releasing former ways and starting over, a new love interest, an abrupt change of heart
- **Reversed:** Holding on to something you need to release, emotional immaturity, emotional damage

Two of Cups

- **Upright:** A harmonious union of soulmates, balance and respect in a new, promising relationship
- **Reversed:** Dishonesty and distrust, a damaged relationship

Three of Cups

- **Upright:** A relationship-centered celebration, lavishness, fertile, feminine energy
- **Reversed:** Addiction, particularly to alcohol, wasteful, overindulgent

Four of Cups

- **Upright:** Losing opportunities because of withdrawing, withdrawing for healthy or unhealthy reasons, boredom
- **Reversed:** Taking an opportunity, breaking a cycle of complacency, acting

Five of Cups

- **Upright:** Mourning, focus on the positives of what is left, regretful, needing to move forward
- **Reversed:** Healthy grief, moving forward after a loss, optimism

Six of Cups

- **Upright:** Wistful reminiscence, fond memories, in touch with your inner child
- **Reversed:** Living in the past, denying your inner child, leaving where you were raised

Seven of Cups

- **Upright:** Grand dreams both achievable and unachievable, dreams but no action, knowing what aspirations are practical and what are not
- **Reversed:** Pursuing one realistic goal, lacking focus, disorganized

Eight of Cups

- **Upright:** Escape, moving on from a relationship that no longer serves you, choosing your contentment first
- **Reversed:** Remaining in a relationship or situation that is not good for you anymore, faking contentment for others, refusing to move on

Nine of Cups

- **Upright:** Seeing the positive results of your work, wealth, bounty
- **Reversed:** A hole in your life, discontentment or dissatisfaction with your life and your accomplishments

Ten of Cups

- **Upright:** A grand celebration, especially concerning family, financial security
- **Reversed:** Discord within family, arguments, losing touch with loved ones

Page of Cups

- **Upright:** Good news, a new love interest, fresh inspiration, more opportunities ahead
- **Reversed:** Emotionally immature, attention-seeking, negligent

Knight of Cups

- **Upright:** A romantic artist, an empath, someone who enriches and inspires
- **Reversed:** Emotionally unstable, jealous, no follow-through

Queen of Cups

- **Upright:** Emotionally intuitive, empathetic, control of emotions
- **Reversed:** Avoiding emotional messages, disharmony between the heart and brain, emotionally exhausted

King of Cups

- **Upright:** In control of emotions, empathetic, intuitive, good decision-making skills
- **Reversed:** Emotionally immature, volatile, oversensitive, withdrawn, poor decision-making skills

Ace of Pentacles

- **Upright:** Manifesting wealth, financial gain, stability
- **Reversed:** Greedy, impoverished, loss of money, missing a good opportunity

Two of Pentacles

- **Upright:** The balance of several unique interests and responsibilities, a call to choose one focus in order to succeed
- **Reversed:** Poor balance of responsibilities, distracted, losing money

Three of Pentacles

- **Upright:** Working well in a group, material achievements from good teamwork, using a team for success
- **Reversed:** Not working well with others, choosing to work solo, the failure of a team

Four of Pentacles

- **Upright:** Setting healthy financial boundaries, stingy, withholding money
- **Reversed:** Overly generous leading to overspending and overindulgence, liberal with money to a fault

Five of Pentacles

- **Upright:** Impoverished or fear of becoming impoverished, losing sight of the blessings you do have, worrying over money, anxiety over money
- **Reversed:** Surviving financial struggles, recovering from financial loss, losing sight of blessings because you are so focused on money

Six of Pentacles

- **Upright:** Truly selfless, receiving charity or being generous, sharing
- **Reversed:** Stingy, greedy, controlling

Seven of Pentacles

- **Upright:** Patience, staying the path, long-term and well-planned goals
- **Reversed:** Short-term goals but no long-term plans, lack of follow-through, distracted

Eight of Pentacles

- **Upright:** Another step toward financial success, reaping the benefits of hard work, ambition, committed to a goal, excellent follow-through
- **Reversed:** Turning down good opportunities, lazy, no follow-through, cutting corners

Nine of Pentacles

- **Upright:** Financial gain due to hard work, material stability, solid investment(s)
- **Reversed:** Bad investment(s), no planning leading to financial instability and loss

Ten of Pentacles

- **Upright:** Inheritance, affluence, generational wealth
- **Reversed:** Familial divides over money, momentary success followed by financial loss

Page of Pentacles

- **Upright:** Planning for the future, new learning opportunity, fresh goals
- **Reversed:** Lacking responsibility and planning, having no prospects

Knight of Pentacles

- **Upright:** Living up to your responsibility, feeling stuck, hard work
- **Reversed:** Irresponsible, refusing to put in the work, slothful

Queen of Pentacles

- **Upright:** Matriarch, financially secure, breadwinner, warm, affectionate
- **Reversed:** No balance of work and home life, financially unstable, independent, taking care of yourself

King of Pentacles

- **Upright:** Wise, wealthy, businessperson, caretaker
- **Reversed:** Ruthless businessperson, successful but cruel, poor

Ace of Swords

- **Upright:** A mental breakthrough, having a vision, seeing clearly
- **Reversed:** Confusion, clouded judgment, angry

Two of Swords

- **Upright:** Stuck in the middle, a decision without all the information, questions of loyalty
- **Reversed:** Deceit, taking sides, seeing clearly

Three of Swords

- **Upright:** Bitterness, deceitfulness, heartbreak
- **Reversed:** Healing after loss, reconciling, self-resentment

Four of Swords

- **Upright:** Beneficial rest, peace, withdrawing
- **Reversed:** Overworked, exhaustion, a need for rest that is refused

Five of Swords

- **Upright:** Argumentative, hopeless, anxious
- **Reversed:** Reconciling, remorseful, therapeutic

Six of Swords

- **Upright:** Maturing, taking time away, leaving a negative situation
- **Reversed:** Stuck but resistant to change, not progressing forward

Seven of Swords

- **Upright:** Lies, stealing, and deceiving
- **Reversed:** Developing a conscience, remorse, atonement

Eight of Swords

- **Upright:** Having no control, difficulty in knowing what's right
- **Reversed:** Autonomy, independence, freedom of constraints

Nine of Swords

- **Upright:** Nightmare, extreme anxiety, despair
- **Reversed:** Seeking help, facing fears, coping with anxiety

Ten of Swords

- **Upright:** Deceit, ruin, fatigue, submitting
- **Reversed:** Rock bottom, recovery, improving, restorative

Page of Swords

- **Upright:** Individualism, thirst for knowledge, potential
- **Reversed:** Fear, lack of follow-through, no action, hasty action

Knight of Swords

- **Upright:** Hasty, smart but unwise, fixer
- **Reversed:** Combative, hostile, volatile

Queen of Swords

- **Upright:** Moral, principles, good communication
- **Reversed:** Emotionally immature, irritable, combative

King of Swords

- **Upright:** Virtuous, integrity, leader, self-disciplined
- **Reversed:** Ruthless, vicious, abusive

MAJOR ARCANA

The Fool

- **Upright:** A new life journey, hopeful, beginning something new and unknown
- **Reversed:** No plan, lack of forethought, ignoring risks

The Magician

- **Upright:** A transformation, intellect, mastery, magic
- **Reversed:** Deceit, trickery, con artist

The High Priestess

- **Upright:** Ancient ritual, sacred knowledge, spiritual wisdom, ancestral knowledge
- **Reversed:** Spiritual disconnect, ignoring ritual of ancestors, emotionally stunted

The Empress

- **Upright:** Sensual, divine feminine, fertility, loving yourself
- **Reversed:** No confidence, overindulgent, juvenile, insecure

The Emperor

- **Upright:** Focused, leader, determined, masculine
- **Reversed:** Bully, overbearing, stubborn, not an authority

The Hierophant

- **Upright:** Intelligent, conformist, traditionalist
- **Reversed:** Breaking norms, rebellion, poor leadership

The Lovers

- **Upright:** Honest, healthy, loving relationship
- **Reversed:** A broken relationship, imbalance, disconnect between two people

The Chariot

- **Upright:** A solo journey, success within reach, stay the path
- **Reversed:** Lack of direction, disorganization, impotence

Strength

- **Upright:** Inner strength, bold, daring
- **Reversed:** Inner strength that is forgotten, lack of confidence, accepting a failure

The Hermit

- **Upright:** Spiritual and emotional restoration, separation from society, wisdom
- **Reversed:** Isolated, lonely, needing help

Wheel of Fortune

- **Upright:** Luck, fate, the karmic circle
- **Reversed:** Unlucky, a bad change, or struggles to make a change

Justice

- **Upright:** Karma, harmony, truth
- **Reversed:** Corrupt, treachery, evasion

The Hanged Man

- **Upright:** A pause, embracing the quiet, patience
- **Reversed:** Refusing a break, inflexible, try viewing things from another angle

Death

- **Upright:** Personal growth, transition, transformation
- **Reversed:** Repeating mistakes, afraid to change, persistent

Temperance

- **Upright:** Peaceful, harmonious, tranquility, calmness
- **Reversed:** Discord, imbalance, gluttony, addiction

The Devil

- **Upright:** Temptation, addiction, destructive cycles
- **Reversed:** Breaking addictions and damaging cycles, overcoming addiction, recovering

The Tower

- **Upright:** Sudden change, a need to leave or go down in flames
- **Reversed:** Fear of change, getting dragged down by others, lying to yourself

The Star

- **Upright:** Calmness after a struggle, healing, restorative time
- **Reversed:** Depression, hopeless, loss of faith

The Moon

- **Upright:** Facing fears, examining relationships, confronting darkness
- **Reversed:** Shedding negative relationships and habits, allowing change

The Sun

- **Upright:** Healthiness, born again, high energy
- **Reversed:** Negativity, lazy, unhealthy, bogged down

Judgment

- **Upright:** Freedom, release, huge changes, intuitive decisions
- **Reversed:** Self-destructive thoughts, lack of confidence, trust your intuition

The World

- **Upright:** The completion of a big life cycle, success, harmony, balance
- **Reversed:** Dissatisfaction, blockage of knowledge or emotions, stagnation, failure

STANDARD US/METRIC CONVERSION CHART

VOLUME CONVERSIONS

US Volume Measure	Metric Equivalent
⅛ teaspoon	0.5 milliliter
¼ teaspoon	1 milliliter
½ teaspoon	2 milliliters
1 teaspoon	5 milliliters
½ tablespoon	7 milliliters
1 tablespoon (3 teaspoons)	15 milliliters
2 tablespoons (1 fluid ounce)	30 milliliters
¼ cup (4 tablespoons)	60 milliliters
⅓ cup	90 milliliters
½ cup (4 fluid ounces)	125 milliliters
⅔ cup	160 milliliters
¾ cup (6 fluid ounces)	180 milliliters
1 cup (16 tablespoons)	250 milliliters
1 pint (2 cups)	500 milliliters
1 quart (4 cups)	1 liter (about)

WEIGHT CONVERSIONS

US Weight Measure	Metric Equivalent
½ ounce	15 grams
1 ounce	30 grams
2 ounces	60 grams
3 ounces	85 grams
¼ pound (4 ounces)	115 grams
½ pound (8 ounces)	225 grams
¾ pound (12 ounces)	340 grams
1 pound (16 ounces)	454 grams

INDEX

Note: Page numbers in *italics* indicate recipes. Page numbers in **bold** indicate tarot card meanings.

ABOUT THE AUTHOR

Thea Engst is a cocktail consultant and writer. She is the author of *Drink Like a Bartender* and coauthor of *Nectar of the Gods*, and currently develops recipes for *Motif* magazine, among others. Her work has been featured on *Chronicle* and in *The Boston Globe*, *Eater Boston*, *Boston* magazine, and *Metro Boston*. She received her MFA in writing from Emerson College, and has been studying tarot for seven years. Thea loves drinking Manhattan variations, wandering through cemeteries, and laughing with friends. She lives in Providence, Rhode Island.

Looking for Some Answers?
LET TAROT BE YOUR GUIDE.

150 PROMPTS *for*
SINGLE CARD TAROT WISDOM

THE

ONE
CARD
TAROT
Journal

MARIA SOFIA MARMANIDES

Pick Up or Download Your Copy Today!